D1304546

The
Chicken
Conspiracy

Breaking The Cycle Of Personal Stress And Organizational Mediocrity

Stacie Hagan and Charlie Palmgren

Recovery Communications, Inc.
P.O. Box 19910, Baltimore, Maryland 21211 • (410) 243-8558

For Marian

(you've waited a long time)

Permission to use the illustrations has been granted by Sarah Spalding Minor.

The following permissions to reprint excerpts have been granted:

On page 9, from *The Song of the Bird* by Anthony de Mello, copyright ©
1982 by Anthony de Mello, S.J., used by permission of Doubleday, a
division of Bantam Doubleday Dell Publishing Group, Inc.

On page 16, from the February, March, April 1998 issue of *Forward Day
by Day,* 412 Sycamore St., Cincinnati, OH 45202, used with permission.

On page 79, from *The Transparent Self* by Sidney Jourard, revised edition,
copyright © 1971, John Wiley & Sons, Inc., used by permission of John
Wiley & Sons, Inc., and Antoinette R. Jourard.

On page 125 and page 135, from *Man's Ultimate Commitment* by Henry
Nelson Wieman, copyright © 1958, Southern Illinois University Press, by
permission.

On page 127, [© 1998] Lotus® Development Corporation, used with permission of Lotus Development Corporation; Lotus® is a registered trademark
of Lotus Development Corporation.

On page 129, from *The Little Prince* by Antoine de Saint-Exupéry, copyright
1943 and renewed 1971 by Harcourt Brace & Company, reprinted by permission of the publisher and William Heinemann (a division of Egmont
Children's Books Limited).

On page 134, reprinted with the permission of Simon & Schuster, from
Jonathan Livingston Seagull by Richard Bach, copyright © 1970 by Richard
D. Bach and Leslie Parrish-Bach.

Praise for
The Chicken Conspiracy

"Years ago Walker Percy wrote a book called, *Lost in the Cosmos: The Last Self Help Book.* He was wrong. If he had written this one, he would have been correct. This insightful and easy-to-read book will give the reader deep understanding of the mindset that is necessary before the seven habits can be effectively practiced along the road less traveled."

— **MICHAEL F. MURRAY, TRAINER AND FACILITATOR**

"We have all wondered why people resist change — even changes for the better. Stacie and Charlie have placed a mirror in front of us all. If you or anyone you know has resisted change — big or small — discover why and what to do about it."

— **MICHAEL D. GOLDBERG**
CHAIRMAN AND CHIEF EXECUTIVE OFFICER, ONCARE, INC.

"At last, this book identifies why so many corporate changes fail. I personally started a variety of change initiatives and it wasn't until I understood this book that I found the missing ingredient to successful, sustainable, change. Stacie and Charlie describe the 'glue' that integrates and enables organizational change."

— **LOUIS STRIPLING, FORMER PRESIDENT AND CEO**
ICCA, INC. AND PROFESSIONAL MEDICAL RESOURCES, INC.

"This book is an extremely important tool to help families of alcoholics reach inside and get that courage."

— **TOBY RICE DREWS, AUTHOR,** *GETTING THEM SOBER*

"This book is a must to understand how we build our own vicious cycles and how we can start finding and living from our creative self."

— **ANNE TEACHWORTH,**
FOUNDER AND DIRECTOR, GESTALT INSTITUTE OF NEW ORLEANS/NEW YORK
AUTHOR, *WHY WE PICK THE MATES WE DO!*

"It is easy to find ourselves in every chapter. We can vastly benefit from the authors' clarity, insight and encouragement about not squandering our energy in ways that harm and limit us. As the richness, depth and hope of the authors' ideas unfold, we realize that the possibilities for ascent into freedom, invigoration, balance and creativity are limitless."

— **HANNAH GARRICK, L.C.S.W., L.M.F.T., B.C.D.**
INDIVIDUAL, COUPLES, AND FAMILY THERAPIST AND SPEAKER

"By the simple offering of a new way to look at 'dis-ease' Hagan and Palmgren point the way toward a simple, clear thought process which begins at the beginning, deals with the basics, builds on logic and leads toward creative transformation."

— COTTEN ALSTON, FATHER, NEIGHBOR, MAN ON THE STREET

"I am delighted to have read this book, which is an encapsulation of the work of two people dedicated to making the world a better place through change in human behavior. I applaud this effort to reach the world with their valuable message."

— MARILYN SHAPIRO
PROGRAM MANAGER, AMERICAN MANAGEMENT ASSOCIATION

"An interesting and thought provoking piece. In today's increasingly inter-dependent workplace, the message from Stacie and Charlie can help us be more effective business leaders . . . and help our people to recover their creative potential."

— ROBERT A. ANCLIEN, PARTNER, ANDERSEN CONSULTING

"Those who read into this text the essence of the title page — pursue creative processes and have the courage to follow their better ideas — will reap a rich reward."

— ROBERT W. GALVIN, CHAIRMAN OF THE EXECUTIVE COMMITTEE, MOTOROLA

"I found myself smiling, nodding, crying, laughing and 'ah-ha'ing, at almost every paragraph! The authors bring to light such basic truths that ring loud in my heart and head and have yielded workable methods to my daily challenges. Thank you for so simply, clearly, poignantly, and truthfully giving me new tools to enhance me and my effectiveness and to bring new peace!"

— ANN W. CRAMER
REGIONAL MANAGER, IBM CORPORATE COMMUNITY RELATIONS

"Public education must equip children by nurturing the eagle within. Charlie and Stacie clearly state the dynamic that undermines education and other social programs."

— WILLIAM E. MILLIKEN
FOUNDER AND PRESIDENT, COMMUNITIES IN SCHOOLS, INC.

"All I want to know is how the authors managed to write a book about me!"

— BETTY BARSTOW, MEDICAL UNIVERSITY OF SOUTH CAROLINA

Contents

Acknowledgments

Like many readers, we often turn past the acknowledgment section of a book in our hurry to get to the author's central message. Only now do we understand that books don't occur in a vacuum, and certainly few, if any, represent the exclusive thinking and effort of the authors. Like everything else in the world, a book results from the effort of numerous people. With this in mind, it is impossible to acknowledge all the people who have helped us along the way.

We have deep appreciation for the life and work of Dr. Henry Nelson Wieman, whose thinking and writing are implicit on every page. His insights have formed the basis for much of our own thought. We are also deeply indebted to the work of Dr. Erle Fitz, a psychiatrist who was a pioneer in understanding that much of stress is really an expression of "what's right about us" and not merely a result of what's wrong with us. We want to thank two long-time friends, Del Poling and Mike Murray, each of whom made significant contributions to the development of this work. As director of a counseling center, Del provided an environment that allowed for development and testing of ideas. Mike Murray, President of Creative Interchange Consultants International, pursues parallel efforts to our own in helping people discover the crippling effects of the Chicken Conspiracy. Mike has been an inspiration and constant supporter in the effort to bring our ideas to print.

Special thanks to Betsy White for her marvelous work and attention to detail during final editing. Her comments and insights were critical to helping bring clarity and flow to the manuscript. Thanks also to Sami Palmgren of SynerChange, for her tireless efforts and valuable comments from the very beginning. We want to express our gratitude to The Reverend Emmett Jarrett for taking time from his busy schedule to provide content comments and encouragement.

We are deeply indebted to our SynerChange colleagues Daphne Roels and Johan Roels of the Belgium office, Keijo Halinen and Arto Kuusinen of the Finland office, and Patricia Marshall of the Chicago office for their commentary, friendship, and continuous support to make this book a reality.

Acknowledgments

Finally, we thank our many friends and colleagues for their patience and understanding over the past few years. We also want to thank our families who had to accept our absence during the many hours required for writing and rewriting, editing and re-editing. We appreciate their sacrifice on our behalf.

Appreciation must also be extended to the authors and publishers who so graciously granted permission for use of their materials in this book.

Are you a
Chicken or an **Eagle?**

❑ Are you sick of self-help and business books that really aren't helpful?

❑ Do you ever feel that people don't really know you?

❑ Have you ever felt that if people really knew you, they wouldn't like you?

❑ Do you ever wonder what life is really all about?

❑ Do you ever wonder why people are in such a hurry and going nowhere (like a chicken with its head cut off)?

❑ Do you think someone might be watching you while you read these questions?

❑ Did you just glance around?

❑ Have you ever wanted to be someone else?

❑ Have you ever come to the end of your rope and found it wasn't attached to anything?

❑ Is boredom part of your job description?

❑ Do you dread Monday mornings?

❑ Do you ever feel stress?

How many YES answers did you have? The more there are, the more tightly the Chicken Conspiracy has you caged. To begin learning how to get free, go on to the Introduction.

Introduction

We begin with a story by Anthony de Mello.

A man found an eagle's egg and put it in the nest of a backyard hen. The eaglet hatched with the brood of chicks and grew up with them.

All his life the eagle did what the backyard chickens did, thinking he was a backyard chicken. He scratched the earth for worms and insects. He clucked and cackled. And he would thrash his wings and fly a few feet into the air.

Years passed and the eagle grew very old. One day he saw a magnificent bird far above him in the cloudless sky. It glided in graceful majesty among the powerful wind currents, with scarcely a beat of its strong golden wings.

The old eagle looked up in awe. "Who's that?" he asked. "That's the eagle, the king of the birds," said his neighbor. "He belongs to the sky. We belong to the earth — we're chickens."

So the eagle lived and died a chicken, for that's what he thought he was.

— The Song of the Bird

This book is about eagles and chickens, in a sense.

Anthony de Mello's story provides a poignant analogy for human life. This is a story about us, about you, about any human being striving in some way to be other than who he or she really is. It's about the eagle in each of us and how many of us live our lives, sadly, assuming we're chickens.

In the name of political correctness, please understand that we are not anti-chicken. It's appropriate that a chicken be the best chicken it can be, just as it's right for an eagle to be the best eagle. The problem occurs when an eagle attempts to be a chicken, or a chicken pretends to be an eagle. And in human life, many of us are like the eagle in the story: ignoring our potential for creative flight and conforming to the belief system and constraints of a chicken culture.

This book is about rediscovering the eagle within each one of us — our unique human capacity for creative transformation and growth in all that each of us can know, appreciate, imagine, and do. Each of us is designed from birth to engage in transforming creativity in the same way an eagle is destined, as de Mello says, "to glide

9

gracefully in a cloudless sky." We see glimpses of this eagle from time to time — those meaningful moments in our lives when we discover something new, are excited by the ordinary, reconnect with another human being, contribute our time and talent to something important. Those times when we share the uniqueness of our experience with others, in a way no one else can, are about the eagle, those rare moments when we live according to who we really are, rather than who we think we're supposed to be.

This book is also about chickens. It's about the false persona that masks our true creativity and identity. It's about the games we play to fit in, be accepted, be successful, about the societal norms that we accept unthinkingly and permit to control our thoughts about what is popular, attractive, and true. It's about the self-concept we construct in an effort to please others and be recognized as interesting or valuable. This book is about how we as parents, teachers, or organizational leaders unwittingly groom others and ourselves to conform to chickenhood. It's about how we, intending good, nevertheless mass-produce mediocrity by forcing or coaxing others into a mold that is premeasured, prepackaged, and predesigned to serve the status quo.

Most of all, this book is about the process that begins in infancy through which we gradually convince ourselves that we're chickens rather than eagles. It's about the process, which, over time, conditions human life for mediocrity rather than creativity, for wearing a persona rather than being a person. Through this process we exchange our original creative selves for ordinary conventional selves. We construct and maintain cages or habits that prevent the soaring flights of creative self in favor of remaining securely grounded like any good barnyard chicken.

This process often leaves us feeling self-conscious, inadequate, and unworthy. Buying into it leads to increasing stress and varied physical complaints. Relationships suffer, productivity declines, and overall satisfaction with self and life deteriorate. These results occur because living into chickenhood when one is designed to be an eagle is a falsehood — one that we struggle to overcome whenever we seek to prove to ourselves and others that we are smart, beautiful, valuable, and worthy. It is false because it denies the nature of the eagle within — our capacity to engage in creativity.

For some readers, this may look like a psychology book, although we provide no therapeutic techniques. The first few chapters may suggest a parenting or child-development book, yet we claim no expertise in these domains. The later chapters might seem designed for business and industry, although the book is not restricted to this field. Quite simply, this book is about all of these and much more. It's a book about people from all walks of life. We tell a story of human striving that applies to everyone, regardless of gender, culture, socio-economic status, or field of expertise.

This is not necessarily a "feel good" book. It describes a human drama that plays out every day to varying degrees in our lives — a process that keeps us from becoming most fully who we are. This drama, with its implications for psychological, spiritual, and physical well-being, invites the reader into a close examination of self. As most adults know, major insights into self are often gained through discomfort, and feeling good all of the time is an unrealistic expectation to place on human life. On the other hand, feeling bad all of the time is not complete human living, either, which is why we wrote this book. So many people today feel unfulfilled, lost, unsatisfied — even when by all accounts they "have everything" and are living out society's version of success. As we describe the process that leads to this emptiness with the fullness of detail we currently understand, we do so believing that liberation from it begins with knowledge and understanding.

We begin our story in the earliest years of life and continue through adulthood. This developmental span is covered, not to offer child-development theories or parenting advice, but instead to illustrate the way the process begins to form and take root in human life. You will recognize people you know as you read these pages. You may recognize yourself. And if you do, then laugh at yourself; laugh with all of us about the silly things we do. In moving toward a deeper understanding of the implications of our actions, in becoming able to see what inhibits us from becoming most fully who we are, we can begin to escape the conspiracy's confining grip.

In essence, this book is about hope — the hope that you and other readers will find the courage to look into the face of the fears that inhibit, become able to claim your worth as a human being, and experience anew the exhilaration of free flight.

Unconditionally,
Stacie and Charlie

Part 1

Playing Chicken:

From Creativity to Conformity

1

Life's Great Illusion

*"My assumption is that the story of any one of us
is in some measure the story of us all."*

— Frederick Buechner

---

*The buildings were old, the majority of the faculty traditional,
the student body a little above average academically, and my
experience and background somewhat out of line for instructing a course in abnormal psychology. Sitting in front of me
was a group of astute students in a midwestern medical school.
I was not highly educated for the position I found myself in;
nevertheless, I had always wanted to teach, and now I had
my chance. To complicate the situation, on this particular day
I was sharing my self-analysis.*

*In those days anyone preparing to work in the field of
psychiatry or psychotherapy was expected to have under-
gone personal analysis before trying to help others with their
own analysis. I had been involved in my personal analysis
with the chief of psychiatry and the head psychologist. They
were opposites when it came to understanding abnormal
human behavior — which probably complicated my journey
through analysis. At least, I like to think it was their approach
and not my psyche that made the road toward insight and
understanding so long. The good news was that the chief of
psychiatry was not your stereotypical academician or psychiatrist. Because he was a man far ahead of his time, many
viewed him as abnormal.*

*The room was overcrowded and stuffy for the early morning
class. The course was certainly not a favorite of sophomore*

medical students. Psychiatry was then, as it still is for many medical students, an undesired requirement for graduation.

On this particular day I risked sharing my psychological observations of myself with the class in order to give them a real example of the theories they were studying. I became a "flasher" — at least from a psychological perspective. My anxiety level was high. At several interludes in the presentation, I wanted to pause, say "never mind," and exit the stage.

I wish I could say that my feelings of nervousness and overexposure were immediately eased by a standing ovation, or at least a rousing round of applause. Instead, upon completion of the presentation, I was met with an overwhelming silence that filled every inch of the room. Some people were staring at what I had written on the board, while others simply stared into space.

Although it seemed like hours, after a few moments the students realized the session was complete and began gathering their notebooks and materials to leave. As I watched my shoes shuffle and moved toward gathering my own things, I was met with the biggest surprise of the day. Several of the students came to me and said that I hadn't just been telling my story. They said it was also their story. The stories differed only in the details, not in the fundamental underlying dynamics. They explained that the silence was a moment of absorption for the insights on life, their own and others, that they had just gained. I knew then that something important had happened in that room, although I was still unclear what it all meant and where it would lead.

Since that day in the classroom 30 years ago that story has been shared hundreds of times in many different settings with many different audiences. The story has been retold to audiences within corporations, public and private schools, churches, synagogues, mosques, government agencies, neighborhood civic groups, high schools and many others. The result that astounds us to this day is that with each retelling of the story, the audience response is the same: "That's not just your story. It's mine as well."

Now, we share it with you. The story is about the simplest and most profound quality of human life — our worth. To every individual who picks up this book and reads these sentences (and, even for those who don't) we say, "You have worth." We are confident of that, even though we've not met you. We need no evidence. We need nothing more. We believe that you are a person of worth. Think about that. How do you feel?

When we introduce this important human characteristic in front of a group, we often receive blank stares or puzzled expressions from the audience. It's as if they don't understand the meaning or relevance of the statement. Certainly, they don't grasp the magnitude of the message or its significance. It's a simple statement: "You have worth." It sounds harmless enough, doesn't it? Nevertheless, the failure on the part of most people to experience their own worth is at the very core of a whole host of human dilemmas and problems.

Sharing this story through the years, we are continually confronted with new examples of how the inability to accept our own worth impacts lives. Apparently no one is completely immune to this threat. It infects all people from all walks of life. In a recent interview with Dotson Rader of *Parade Magazine,* David Letterman, one of the stars of late-night TV, shared the ongoing struggle that consumes him with every performance: "Every night you're trying to prove your self-worth . . . You want to be the absolute best, wittiest, smartest, most charming, best smelling version of yourself . . . " Keep in mind, this is David Letterman — a man most Americans would regard as highly successful. Letterman's description of the talk-show-host experience is not unlike daily human experience. Consider the following statement from a less familiar American:

> Most of my life, I've been pretty insecure about who I am and, consequently have spent my energy trying to impress others and present my continuously-up-dated, what-I-think-will-make-me-acceptable-in-your-eyes image of myself.
>
> — Author unknown, *Forward Day by Day*

A contributor to a booklet for daily reflections provided this parallel to Letterman's statement, writing from the confines of his prison cell, where he is serving a life sentence for manslaughter.

Although the extreme difference in life circumstances coupled with the very similar daily battles experienced by these two men is striking, perhaps most notable is their ability to articulate so clearly the human struggle to acknowledge worth. It is a struggle familiar to all of us. The degree to which we understand the struggle and allow ourselves to be controlled by it differs from individual to individual.

By worth we do not mean self-esteem, self-image, or self-concept as popularly understood. Many people are heavily invested in today's fads and those pop psychologies intended to boost self-esteem. While many of these programs are well intentioned, they often perpetuate the myth that personal worth derives from what we do (performance), who we are (position), or whom we know or impress (prestige). The underlying assumption is that worth is bestowed by something or someone outside ourselves. This is life's great illusion.

Vance Packard summarized the situation well in *The Hidden Persuaders*. Writing about the fields of advertising and marketing, he argued that the best in the business could "Get people to buy things they don't want, at a price they can't afford, to impress people they don't like." Our point is not to analyze the ethics of today's advertising methods, but to see that we *are* the people who fall prey to this mentality! Why? Where did "keeping up with the Joneses" begin, and why does this competitive need control our lives?

In contemporary culture, the pursuit of ever-greater achievements has become the hallmark of success and basis for proving one's worth, as the familiar bumper sticker declares: "The one who dies with the most toys wins." It is this perpetual pursuit of ego stroking that many of us confuse with gaining authentic personal worth. Whether in school, on the job, at the athletic field, or in the concert hall, conventional wisdom applauds *worth through performance*. Certainly there is value in high performance, achievement, creativity, and productivity. Striving to learn and do our best is a value to uphold, not criticize. The deeper difficulty stems from the unchallenged illusion that a person's worth is somehow irretrievably attached to such performance outcomes.

The struggle to gain a sense of worth from the outside is not limited to any particular age group or socio-economic class. The endless race for upward mobility through competition, accumulation, and conspicuous consumption is only one aspect of the story. The same striving for worth occurs in the teenager pursuing gang membership, the ten-year-old demanding designer clothes or becoming anorexic to fit an ideal image, or an elderly person fighting feelings of uselessness and the depression of loneliness.

Listen up! A fundamental reason why we resist change, work desperately to gain control of our lives, and experience stress, anxiety, and a variety of psychological and physical difficulties is that we are unable to perceive, experience, and accept our own worth as persons. A deeply rooted illusion lies at the foundation of human personality development. This illusion is the cause of more human suffering and wasted human potential than anything else known to humankind, and it is a pervasive illusion. Hope arises, however, once we realize that it is only an illusion.

In the pages that follow, we describe how this great illusion enters and establishes residence in human life. We explore the impact of this illusion on personal growth and learning, on the ability to develop and maintain healthy constructive relationships, and on the ability to lead, create, and produce in the corporate world.

We invite you to explore these applications further by reflecting on the questions at the end of each chapter, which are designed to assist you in making connections to your own life. For many, this book is best read slowly, allowing time for reflection after each chapter. We encourage you to take your time while reading. The initial step in recognizing the illusion that has the power to imprison is understanding how the cage is constructed from the beginning.

2

Discovering What We Never Lost

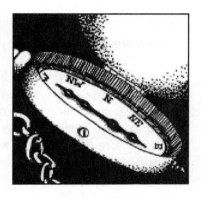

I've been searching for something
Taken out of my soul.
Something I'd never lose
Something somebody stole . . .

— Billy Joel, "River of Dreams"

Dave and Susan just had their first baby. The past year was a whirlwind for them. Both successful attorneys in well-established law firms, they took a dream vacation to Ireland to be married and honeymoon. Three months later, they discovered they had a baby on the way. Dave and Susan both wanted children — some day. The surprise was that "some day" came sooner than they thought.

Being competent, well-organized individuals, they recovered from the shock quickly and moved immediately into preparations. The months of waiting were filled with remodeling and redecorating, transforming the makeshift office/guestroom into a nursery worthy of a magazine cover. Their efforts expanded to a complete transformation of the adjacent bathroom as well — whether a newborn infant would use it or not.

With the perfect home in order, it was time for the perfect baby to arrive. And perfect she was. Ten fingers, ten toes, beautiful eyes and a head full of hair! The entire family was the picture of perfection — until they brought their daughter home.

Every two hours, this child demands to eat, twenty-four hours a day. Dave and Susan attempt to take shifts at night, but it is futile. Dave isn't much help, needing rest since he tries to go to work each day. Susan is taking a short leave and maintains client contacts by phone — at least theoretically. Every time she dials the number of a client, the baby is ready to be fed, needs a diaper change, has a stomach ache, or otherwise cries out for attention. Not much is getting done.

Exhausted and tripping over boxes of disposable diapers and formula, Dave picks up the baby for one last "kiss from Dad" before heading off to work. He's due for a court appearance in less than 30 minutes. As he smiles and talks to his new baby, she reintroduces him to her last bottle of formula — over the shoulder and down the lapel of his best navy suit.

Question: "Mom, Dad, how's it going?"

Dad, dressed in navy and spit-up, and Mom, in tousled hair and bathrobe, dark circles under her eyes and looking less than professional, say in unison, "She's the most wonderful thing that ever happened to us."

If worth is based on performance, newborn infants are a questionable commodity. Every newborn child spends the first few weeks of life establishing a pretty sloppy track record. The necessary biological functions are beyond control and require the nearly constant care and attention of someone else. The newcomer causes the parents numerous sleepless nights and otherwise disrupts the entire household. Totally dependent on others for survival, what could this baby possibly be good for? If worth is unequivocally tied to performance capabilities, the newborn infant is worse than worthless.

Yet the universal cry goes up: "Of course the newborn child is worth something! Every one is worth a great deal!" We hear these comments all the time, even though we all agree, that by most standards for determining worth or value in another human being, crying and making a scene whenever things are less than perfect, spitting up food, and soiling one's undergarments are usually not on the list. So, what *is* worth?

For the Muslim, the Jew, or the Christian, human worth is rooted in the Genesis story of creation, which affirms that people are made in God's image and that God has indicated that all creation is valuable. Other religious views, humanists, and New Age gurus suggest that all people are children of the universe and that each of us has an innate right to exist or be. This innate right assumes the intrinsic value or worth of persons.

We believe that **human worth is the capacity to participate in transforming creativity.** Human worth is our potential to continually expand what any one of us can know, appreciate, imagine, and do. We were designed especially for this transformative process — just as the eagle was designed for flight. The ability to learn, grow, change, develop, imagine, and discover is what constitutes our human worth and fulfills the purpose of our design. While our worth originates in this capacity, we live out of our worth by engaging in transforming creativity. In this way, human worth is about both "being" and "doing."

Worth Is Inherent

Regardless of where worth originates, the simple conclusion is that we all have it. Worth is innate. At the biological level, the premise that worth is innate is simple to test. Let us describe the experiment. One person — the subject — will lie on the floor. The other persons cover the subject's mouth and hold the nose closed for eight minutes. We predict that within a minute there will be a noticeable change in the subject's behavior. The subject will tend to become more aggressive — perhaps even violent — in the effort to uncover nose and mouth. The change in behavior will include any action that might preserve life. The change in behavior is a goal-seeking activity, demonstrating that we are programmed to sustain life.

Obviously we don't recommend that you gather your friends and try this — it could be a good way to lose friends! The point is that your own body, without you instructing it, has a biological sense of worth. Why would you fight to stay alive if there were no reason to do so? You react physically to this threat because life, your life, is worth preserving. Unless one is suffering from severe emotional and physical problems that make life intolerable, we innately know that we are valuable and worth keeping alive.

Worth on the biological level takes the form of this survival need or instinct. Yet this is not the sum total of human worth. Survival goals provide a mere starting point for human beings and are quickly followed by a more advanced goal: namely, the need for creative transformation. Our need for creative transformation is to our psychological and spiritual survival what oxygen, water, food, exercise, and sleep are to physical well-being.

Worth at the psychological and spiritual levels is also a given and is observable in infants. When the diaper is dry, the stomach is full, the room temperature is appropriate and all other physical needs are met, the healthy infant does not merely sleep or slip into a vegetative state. In fact, the opposite occurs. As Dr. Erle Fitz, a noted psychotherapist and friend, has observed, "The newborn child engages in increasing interludes of wakefulness." In other words, when all physical survival needs are met, the child initiates his or her own exploration of the world. The child begins to watch, interact, and otherwise seek understanding of the outside world. Why? Human beings are designed for this type of evolution or development. This continual development or expansion enables us to understand, influence, and find meaning in our world. In this way, human beings are designed for creative transformation in the same way that the eagle is designed for flight. Even in our earliest days, even with the worst behavior or performance, we have worth. We contend that this capacity for creative transformation defines human worth. You are a human being of worth. Worth is a constant. Your worth is unconditional. In truth, your worth is a given.

You never have been and you never will be worth more than you are right now. You are worth all you can be worth at this very moment.

How do those statements make you feel? Do they make you squirm a bit? Read them again. Think about them again. If worth (your capacity to engage in transforming creativity) is a given, then your worth accompanied you into this world. Therefore, your performance in any area has nothing to do with establishing worth, and nothing you have ever done caused you to lose your worth, just as nothing you will ever do will gain more worth for you.

Of course, you may have greater financial worth than you once had, or you may have more skills, more knowledge, and more experience that enables you to act more effectively and efficiently than you once did. You may also gain new wealth, skills, or knowledge in the future. But, regardless of past progress or failure and future plans, worth is constant. Contrary to popular belief, your human worth has nothing to do with what you accumulate in the way of financial wealth, academic degrees, houses or cars owned, or honors achieved. Human worth is not subject to the whims of the stock market, applause, or the accolades of others.

While the capacity to engage in transforming creativity is innate, this does not mean that we all possess or use this capacity to the same degree. Because worth is innate, even those who behave violently and destructively against others have worth. In the case of heinous crimes such as rape or murder, acknowledgment of the perpetrator's worth is not easy. Yet it is important for us to understand and accept worth as a given. A criminal's behavior can blind us to that person's worth. Perhaps the criminal's worth has been so severely attacked that he or she attacks others in self-defense. While we do not justify criminal acts, the point remains that performance can neither add to nor diminish human worth.

Consider the young child who acts out violently and perhaps even sexually at school. Further investigation into the child's background and home life reveals that he is a victim of physical and sexual abuse. After removal from the abusive situation and appropriate therapeutic intervention, the child is able to cope with the problems, and the inappropriate behavior subsides. With loving support and nurturing caregivers, a gentle personality emerges. In the absence of intervention, this same child might have grown into an abusive adult, reenacting his own abuse with others. Regardless of the scenario, the question remains the same. Have these actions proved him — the adult or the child — to be without worth? Or was worth always there, even when not actualized through appropriate behavior?

Experiencing Worth

The core issue is not whether we have worth, but whether we have a consistent *experience* of it. This experience of worth is central to developing a healthy identity. Yet most of us lose touch with it — just like the eagle in de Mello's story. The eagle is designed for flight. It has an inclination to fly, and the eagle's worth is actualized through flight. When the eagle's erroneous belief that it's a chicken obstructs its inclination for flight, then the eagle's experience of its value or worth is diminished.

In the same manner, human beings experience their greatest fulfillment and satisfaction through transforming creativity. These pivotal moments come in large and small packages. They are sometimes anxiously awaited, as one awaits the birth of a child, or as one arrives at completion of a goal that stretched you and helped you discover what you're truly capable of. They are often abruptly experienced, as one learns of the sudden, unexpected loss of a loved one. At other times they enter our lives through a whisper and leave us speechless — as when we are caught breathless by the beauty of autumn leaves or see the love and trust in a small child's eyes. The moment is unmistakable. We are forever changed. These are the moments in life when insights come, discoveries are made, and everything becomes new.

When we engage in this transforming creativity, we experience the satisfaction of living out our worth. When we submit to living in ways that obstruct this capacity, we experience dissatisfaction or dis-ease. However difficult it may sometimes be to acknowledge, ultimately, we always have a choice. We can experience the satisfaction of living out our worth, or we can experience the painful ongoing frustration of seeking worth through performance.

Seeking worth through performance is equivalent to the eagle's attempt to live as a chicken. Every time we seek to *earn* worth, we feel the frustration of a great bird born for free flight but bound by the bars of a cage. Because an experience of worth is central to our psychological, emotional, and spiritual health, we can predict the loss of purpose, meaning, and fulfillment in life that occurs when anyone lives for an extended period without experiencing creative transformation. In its efforts to fly, the eagle beats its wings futilely against the constraints of its cage. Likewise, we may spend the rest of our lives continually yet futilely striving to regain worth — the worth we never lost to begin with.

In the pages that follow, we illustrate how this misguided effort to gain worth through performance builds a cage over time that entraps human life.

WORTH

*Worth
is defined by the
capacity to engage in
transforming
creativity.*

*Worth is inherent in
every human being.*

INSIGHT QUESTIONS

Personal Growth:

- Record how you feel about this statement: "You never have been and you never will be worth more than you are right now."

- What performance goals have you believed you must achieve in order to feel good about yourself?

- Think about moments in your life that changed you forever. Record one or two of those examples. How did these situations creatively transform you?

Relationships:

- Consider how your sense of worth is increased or decreased in relationship with others. Describe a relationship that helps you feel good about yourself. How is your experience of your worth nourished by relationship?

- Describe a relationship in which you feel bad about yourself. How is your experience of worth threatened in this relationship?

Organizations:

- What performance criteria do you have for yourself in your career? How do these criteria affect your experience of your worth?

- Does your organization treat people in ways that affirm worth or performance? Think about specific examples. What could be different?

3

Defying Human Nature

> *"Society attacks early, when the individual is helpless."*
> — B.F. Skinner

Alex is a scientist, a true empiricist. He is a keen observer of his environment, always watching, listening, exploring, thinking. He never takes things for granted — never rests on an assumption. Alex doesn't even know what an assumption is. He repeatedly formulates theories, tests them, alters them, and retests. He does this work without ceasing — except, of course, for an occasional nap. You see, Alex is two years old.

It was a typical morning in Alex's lab. Again this morning, like every other morning this week, Alex was studying the relationship between gravity and orange juice. Each previous morning, as he tipped the cup over the edge of his workspace (known to some as the high-chair tray), the juice went down, usually arranging itself in an interesting pattern on the floor. How could he be sure this would happen again today? Only by testing. When you're a scientist, that's what you do.

Alex's managers (a.k.a. Mom and Dad) were losing patience with their little scientist. Dad's slippers became glued securely to the kitchen floor this morning as he made his way to the coffeepot. Mom had scrubbed this mess one time too many to worry about being thorough today. It was kind of cute the first day. Now it was definitely getting old. The words "No! No!" seemed to have little impact.

Just as the juice began its second descent of the morning, Mom slammed down her coffee cup and yelled in a sharp voice, "That's it, Alex! I've had it with this little stunt." Alex caught a glimpse of the furrowed brow and the angry eyes glaring at him just before his father scooped him out of the high chair and took him to his room. "Breakfast is over, young man!" he roared. "We're not tolerating that any more." And he stormed out of the room.

Alex sat motionless in the middle of the floor, his lower lip protruding and his eyes filling with tears. The great experiment had ended. And he was still hungry. More importantly, he was alone.

The process of conditioning a child has many names — socialization, enculturation, domestication, early childhood development, or just plain child rearing. Regardless of what the process is called, it is a hazardous journey under the best of conditions. It's hazardous to the caregivers, who often question whether they're doing the right thing. And it's hazardous to the child being socialized, who is trying to understand what the "right thing" is.

Barring serious illness or birth defect, children enter the world as ravenous learners. Like our eagle, the child is eager to soar majestically with a sense of wonder and curiosity for the world. From its first day, an infant absorbs massive amounts of information and experience. Every child begins to form concepts of people and things, good and bad — an infinite variety. Children continually test these conceptual frameworks and refine them to improve accuracy. In short, children enter the world innately knowing how to learn. They enter the world engaging in transforming creativity.

Because discovering and testing boundaries is a primary motivator for children, they often do things adults wish they wouldn't. Our task, then, is to guide or channel the child's curiosities through the maze of ambiguity into areas that are safe and socially acceptable. This is the earliest stage at which the eagle's instincts encounter the pecking order of "chickenhood" — when the child begins to learn about acceptable and unacceptable behavior.

So what is the right thing to do? What is socially acceptable? Our diverse culture provides a plethora of confusing answers. Most notions about effective parenting seem to be directed toward one common end: children must be taught limits in order to understand how society functions and how they are expected to function within that society. Parents and other caregivers become the bridge between complete freedom and socially acceptable behavior.

But suppose you're the child, and you don't have all these societal norms carefully alphabetized and categorized in your head. How do you discover them? Unfortunately, we live in a society that allocates more attention towards "wrong" behaviors than towards "right." Our evening news is filled with the awful things people do and is nearly void of the wonderful things that happen every day. Our educational system typically emphasizes, by red marks, the items on the child's exam that are wrong rather than the ones that are correct. Generally, we tell people what not to do and assume that sooner or later they will somehow stumble upon the desirable behavior.

In such a society, the child and everyone else learns society's rules or pecking order by discovering what not to do — by making mistakes. Alex had a quick lesson in what not to do this morning. He learned that when he pours his orange juice on the floor, he loses his breakfast. This may not be so serious. Another meal or snack will likely come along soon. Of greater impact was the other lesson Alex learned, which is that when he pours his orange juice on the floor, people make mean angry faces at him, put him in a room by himself, and go away. Alex has experienced rejection — the arch-enemy of worth. Rejection works against his innate drive for transforming creativity, because when he exercises it, the important people in his world do not appreciate his efforts.

"This is just the way life is," you may be thinking. But consider the situation from the child's perspective. The child is completely dependent on those adults for survival. Without them, there is no food, no home, no clothing, no protection whatsoever. Being abandoned by these adults, even if only for a five-minute "time out" in the bedroom, can be perceived as very threatening. Unfortunately, rejection in the form of neglect has proven this point on many occasions when small children are left alone only to die in a fire, drown in a neighbor's swimming pool, or be abused by a baby-sitter.

If you're reading this book, you were sufficiently valued by others to allow for your physical survival. And if your parents knew that children learn and grow best in positive and nurturing environments, they did their utmost to provide such an environment. Even for Alex, his parents will likely use desirable parenting techniques, being careful to say not that Alex is unacceptable, only that his *behavior* is unacceptable. Nevertheless, even with the best parental intentions, the child's *interpretation* of the situation governs the message delivered about worth.

Rejection's Consequences

A child who has experienced rejection is relatively easy to detect. For adults, identifying the fall-out is more difficult. Children respond in universal ways to rejection. Regardless of culture, gender, socio-economic status, etc., the response to rejection is the same. It usually begins with a protruding lower lip, then a downward gaze, followed by erratic breathing. And there is often a little tear running down the cheek. You don't have to touch or otherwise physically harm a child to elicit this response. Yet the pain of rejection runs just as deep as the pain of physical assault. The pain runs deep because rejection is a statement about the conditionality of one's worth. The rejection message is clearly delivered in other ways: the pursuit of "eagleness" is not appreciated in a chicken society.

Through rejection, Alex comes to believe that his worth is conditional. As he sits on his bedroom floor, reflecting on his situation, preparing to cry, he probably does not draw a conscious conclusion that he lacks worth. Rather, he has learned that "when I do some things, people smile and laugh and want to play with me. This is good. When I do other things, they make angry faces, yell at me, and leave me alone. This is bad." Perhaps less consciously, his conclusion becomes, "There are parts of me that are good and there are parts of me that are bad."

How many times have well-meaning parents told their children, "Be good and I will bring you a treat"? This implies that the child has the potential to "be" bad, rather than just "act" bad, and suggests to the child that she keep her "badness" under wraps. This is in no way meant to be accusatory of parents. We're both parents, and we've said these things to our own children.

Even a rejecting look on our faces is enough to send the message that worth is conditional. I realized this when my own two-year-old daughter came to sit on my lap after I had scolded her. She placed her little finger on my forehead and attempted to smooth out my furrowed brow. She wanted me to be pleased with her. The message was clear — rejection is experienced as a break in relationship.

We certainly are not suggesting that children be allowed to run wild without regard for how their actions might affect others or endanger themselves. Children need limits; carefully choosing the manner in which we impose those limits is important. We find great value in parenting techniques that avoid terms such as "being bad" or "being good," resorting instead to describing *behaviors* as useful and constructive, or damaging and destructive. These are good tips to follow and provide tools for correcting dangerous behavior while staying in relationship.

At some point in everyone's life, children and adults will experience rejection. One mother took her four-year-old daughter to the grocery store for the weekly shopping. The daughter decided that she wanted — no, *needed* — a particular piece of candy. The mother denied the request. The child dropped to the floor and began kicking, screaming, and attracting a great deal of attention. The mother immediately stepped back into the circle of onlookers and commented, "Whose child is that?" While the mother could have chosen other more negative or abusive responses, it remains likely that the child experienced the conditionality of her worth in the familiar form of rejection.

When we do something to which others respond negatively, we experience rejection of the behavior, of ourselves for having engaged in it, and of our worth for evoking the disappointment of others. Because we can't ultimately eliminate our innate worth, rejection puts us into a painful conflict. When we meet with rejection, we feel discomfort, for our very psychological health is dependent on experiencing our worth as persons. Momentary rejection might not be so painful if it weren't for the resulting, long-term distortion of our sense of worth. In keeping with our eagle, we become trapped in the struggle to deny "eagleness" and pretend "chickenness." This core conflict is at work in all of us. We are all kept very busy denying our creative selves in favor of striving to build an inauthentic constructed self.

WORTH

REJECTION
Conditional
Worth

Through experiences of rejection, we accept our worth as conditional and dependent on behaving appropriately and pleasing others.

INSIGHT QUESTIONS

Personal Growth:

- Think of some of the ways in which you have experienced rejection. What emotions did you feel? Which ones did you express?

- Why can't you feel good in the midst of rejection?

Relationships:

- In what ways have you rejected others this week? Although you may not have intended to place conditions on that person's worth, how might they have perceived your act as a rejection of worth?

- How have you experienced rejection by others this week? In what ways did you negate your worth in these situations?

Organizations:

- How do people in your organization experience rejection? Make a list of potential scenarios.

- What forms of actual or implied rejection does your organization use?

4

The Chemistry of Survival

*"For fast-acting relief,
try slowing down."*

— Lily Tomlin

It was a brisk fall morning. In fact, it was gorgeous! The sun was shining, and the leaves were nearly at their peak of autumn color. With a cup of hot coffee in his hand, George took a deep breath of the cool air and climbed in the car to begin the office commute.

He enjoyed the scenery as he drove. After a good night's sleep, he felt energized and convinced that he was about to begin a highly productive day. Even this morning's drive could be productive. Why not start now? George began to think through the various projects, meetings, phone calls, and other tasks that he would complete by day's end. With some careful planning, they might even be done by noon!

His mind was a whir as he changed lanes, left the interstate, and entered the major thoroughfare that led to his office complex.

It all happened in a flash. In the middle of the intersection, George was jolted by an image in the corner of his eye of a large truck barreling toward him from the right, inches, it seemed, from his passenger door. Almost instinctively, he stomped on the gas and escaped a collision. "I had the right-of-way! What were they thinking! They had a red light!" Thoughts raced through George's mind.

Less than a block later, George felt a physical rush so overpowering that he was forced to pull the car to the side *of the road. The office was only a half mile farther, but George's forehead was covered with sweat, and his hands were shaking. Glancing in the mirror, he saw that his face had lost all color.*

Throughout the day, whenever George remembered the near-collision, these same feelings came back — not as intense as the first time, but recognizable nevertheless. It left a sick feeling in his stomach.

Welcome to the chemistry of survival. You've probably been in this situation yourself: a near-miss while driving, catching yourself just before you fall, or being frightened by a friend who enjoys jumping out from around the corner and scaring you silly. The rush of chemicals washing through the body is undeniable.

Actually, it's a good thing they exist. These chemicals are part of a complex alerting process called the General Adaptation Syndrome, more commonly known as the fight-or-flight response. The response involves an immediate and massive change in the body's biochemistry, alerting us to potential threat and equipping us for immediate and focused action. The body is energized so that we can either fight or flee, to remain safe.

When the fight-or-flight response is triggered, heart and respiratory rates rise. Awareness heightens. Adrenaline is released, and blood is pumped to the areas of the body that need it most. You may have heard stories of a mother lifting an object many times her own weight in order to save her small child trapped beneath. This powerful chemical reaction enables us to do things we never thought possible.

As our human species has evolved, the General Adaptation Syndrome has played an important role in our survival. The immediate response patterns are associated with the reptilian portion of the brain, preceding higher cortical functions such as reasoning and logic. If you are being pursued by a saber-toothed tiger, it's surely more important to be running and hiding than working out the logical consequences of being caught. Fast action or delay determined whether a Stone Age person got lunch or became lunch!

In George's case, the chemicals released enabled him to escape death or at least severe injury. The "rush" he experienced was part of his body's response to the onslaught of chemicals. Yet even under circumstances far less threatening than a saber-toothed tiger or giant semi in your path, any threat evokes the same "rush."

Anyone who has awakened from a nightmare knows the experience of a pounding heart, sweaty palms, rapid breathing, and pervasive anxiety. Even though reality indicates you are safe in your bed, the dream image of the poisonous snake about to strike can activate the General Adaptation Syndrome as surely as being confronted by an actual poisonous snake in broad daylight. The emotional and physical response of the body is the same. The body makes no distinction between actual threat and perceived threat.

Response To Threats To Our Worth

The same is true for threats against worth as for threats against life — there is no distinction. Consider, for example, the child totally dependent on adult caregivers for survival. Through the years, the child struggles between the desire for immediate gratification and parental restrictions. The child inevitably experiences rejection in some degree as he spontaneously acts upon his desires and is corrected, disciplined, and otherwise managed by the caregiver. Even in these relatively minor episodes of rejection, the threat to worth gets associated with a threat to biological survival and triggers the General Adaptation Syndrome. As a result, the child's response to rejection reflects a response to perceived danger to life. And, as with anything that is repeated continually, over time the resulting response pattern to these threats becomes ingrained in the adult. We begin to understand, then, why rejection in any form triggers such intense responses in us.

The response to rejection is not completely summarized, however, by a racing heart and rapid breathing. We are more than biochemical beings — we also have emotions. We all experience tangled webs of emotions when encountering a threat to life or to worth. In fact, the evoked emotions often remain long after the threat to worth or survival has disappeared. The four basic emotions generated in the response to a threat to survival or to worth are *anger, fear, hurt,* and *guilt.*

Feelings of anger and fear are easily understood in association with the fight-or-flight response. Because we have an innate drive for physical survival, we are angered by threats to that survival and fear the sources of threat. The anger focuses energy for the fight response, while the fear helps us make future choices to avoid dangerous, life-threatening situations.

Physical survival, however, is only part of the story. In addition, each of us has a psychological and spiritual sense of worth and a desire to keep intact our value as creative human beings. Being able to experience our worth is central to the psychological, spiritual, and emotional well-being that typifies a meaningful and purposeful life. Our need for creative transformation is as primal as the need to survive. When worth is attacked, both fear and anger are present because of the association of worth and survival. Thriving psychologically and spiritually are as critical as surviving physically. For this reason, the emotional response to rejection becomes as intense as the emotional response to a threat to physical survival.

To further complicate this dynamic, guilt and hurt are involved. In the struggle of wills between child and caregiver, this complex set of emotions emerges. The child's efforts are frustrated as the adult prevents her from doing exactly as she pleases. A sense of injustice or a perceived lack of fair play accompanies this. The child's need for fair play is associated with right and wrong, and these things involve guilt. In the simple logic of the child, she must not be a completely "good" person because she wants to do or have something that is "bad." Wrongdoing evokes guilt, because it equates with not having worth, or being "bad."

She also feels guilt because she is causing some distress and disappointment in the person whom she holds in high regard and from whom she needs love and support. This stirs feelings of hurt because of the potential or perceived withdrawal of love or being devalued in the eyes of the caregiver. Right/wrong, should/shouldn't are associated with guilt, while hurt is associated with diminished love, acceptance, and perceived worth.

Remember George and the giant semi? George felt angry at the driver of the truck for directly disobeying or ignoring the traffic light. He was most certainly frightened by the experience. Perhaps he even experienced a bit of guilt for thinking about his work schedule instead of focusing completely on his driving. If he took this a bit further, he may have sent such messages to himself as, "You're always trying to do too many things at once. You never focus on where you are and what you're doing. How could you be so stupid! There are people who depend on you! You could have gotten yourself killed!" These self-deprecating statements evoke a deep sense of hurt, because George's worth is under attack — albeit by himself.

In summary, when someone is faced with rejection of worth (or threat to survival), anger, fear, guilt and hurt are triggered and converge to form the basis for socialization. If this seems complicated, it's because it is. Any time you have experienced rejection, you know that the tangle of emotions was not always easy to sort out.

This response is most readily seen in a child. When a child is really angry, its fists clench, and its face turns red. There may be kicking, screaming, and other behaviors adults label as a "temper tantrum." It is also relatively easy to tell when a child is afraid. The child will cower, curl up, back away, and otherwise prepare to protect itself. When the biochemistry of fight-or-flight is present in the child, the child naturally expresses or discharges it immediately. When the child is angry or fearful, it is angry or fearful all over.

While these emotions are less often overtly expressed in adults, they are nonetheless present. The combination of anger, fear, guilt, and hurt constitutes a pattern of emotional response to rejection and a perceived loss of worth that continues into adulthood. It is the experience adults most fear, the one we all attempt to evade at any cost. If this doesn't seem obvious, it's because we adults have learned to alter radically our awareness of these biochemical changes, along with any expression of emotion they produce. We skillfully perform a complex set of maneuvers to help us ignore, evade, or otherwise suppress our emotional response to rejection. So, in the face of rejection, while the behaviors may be absent, the chemistry of survival is still very present.

WORTH

REJECTION
Conditional
Worth

Anger – Fear
Guilt – Hurt

Rejection evokes feelings of anger, fear, guilt, and hurt. These emotions become associated with the fight-or-flight chemistry of survival.

INSIGHT QUESTIONS

Personal Growth:

- Remember a time when you were "in trouble" with a parent, teacher, friend, or boss. What emotions did you feel?

- Which of the four emotions — fear, anger, guilt, and hurt — can you express easily? How do you express them?

Relationships:

- In what relationships do you feel free to express your emotions fully? Why?

- In what relationships do you hide your emotions? Why?

Organizations:

- How are emotions handled in your work organization? Are people encouraged to stifle their emotions or "leave them at home"?

- When an "emotional outburst" occurs at your place of work, how is it handled?

5

An Inadequate Design

"I don't know any parents who look into the eyes of a newborn baby and say, 'How can we screw this kid up?'"

— Russell Bishop

When you're a kid, it's important to know whether you have a five "no" or a seven "no" mommy (or daddy, for that matter).

Pudgy, with big brown eyes and soft brown ringlets of hair, Rachel is a doll! Everyone has to stop and look, remarking to Mom and Dad what a cutie she is. She's one and a half years old and very mobile now. Whether on her knees or feet, she can get to just about anything she wants. It's not so much her physical prowess that determines success; it's her focus and perseverance.

This morning's target is Mother's prize vase in the corner of the living room. Understand, this is not a museum-quality piece; nevertheless, Mom loves it. It's one of her favorite treasures, having been passed down from a great-aunt on the mother's side. Rachel has taken a particular interest in the vase today. It's shiny with little bumpy flowers all over it, and Rachel thinks, "I can't wait to touch that and get it in my mouth and really look it over!" Her mission begins as the drool runs down her chin.

Rachel is toddling across the room looking determinedly at the vase. But Mom is not easily fooled. She's witnessed this scene before. She takes one glance at Rachel and instantly sums up the situation: "No, no, Rachel." (That's one and two.) This has little impact. Rachel is busy. She's on a mission. This is going to be exciting!

Within seconds Rachel hears again, "No, Rachel." (That's three.) This time the voice is a bit louder, firmer, higher pitched, yet still unsuccessful. "I wonder if it will bounce?" Rachel muses as she continues undaunted on her course. Suddenly Rachel hears a familiar phrase in a very stern voice, quite a bit louder this time: "No. No! I'm not going to say it again!" (That's five.)

"Well, thank goodness!" Rachel sighs to herself. "I was tired of hearing you talk! I'm busy, here. I've got things to do, and all that racket you're making is not helping a bit!" Rachel continues full speed ahead, "I'm almost there! I can almost taste it!" Suddenly she is swept up, hears another, angrier "NO! NO!" and feels a sudden pain in her gluteus maximus. (That's the muscle we use for sitting — and that's seven.)

Of course, Rachel is a determined child. With a tear running down one cheek, as she reaches backward and stretches just far enough to get one little touch of the vase, she feels a second quick impact to her backside. Rachel is quickly carted off to another room, her mission unsuccessful and aborted, by no choice of her own.

Rachel and her mother have just engaged in one of hundreds of skirmishes they will participate in over the months and years ahead. It's a war of wills — Rachel's desire to explore (and experience transforming creativity) vs. her mother's will to protect a valued possession, and perhaps protect Rachel from injury.

Rachel is about to enter what is commonly known as the "Terrible Two's." If you have children, you need no definition. If you don't, this is a period when the child's values and desires often clash strongly with those of the parent, other caregivers, and society as a whole. This war of wills is particularly pronounced during these early years of life because the child has yet to understand such concepts as dangerous, hot, sharp, noisy, careless, destructive, and hurtful. With relatively few self-monitoring systems, the child begins each new day with an intent to explore and discover anything that seems of interest. Adults label this period "terrible" because it involves a seemingly endless, massive conditioning process in which the adult struggles to channel the child's drive for creative transformation into conventional conformity. It involves a conversion of the eagle's desire for flight into the confines of the barnyard. This is the time when conditioning away from the creative self towards the constructed self gets fully underway.

Whatever the developmental label, these little battles are stormy. The child asserts himself and tests the parents or other adults. These adults respond with some guidelines for acceptable vs. unacceptable, safe vs. unsafe, and numerous other categories for behaviors. These guidelines serve as limits, conditions, or boundaries, which the child "must not" cross. But of course children do cross them. And, like Rachel, they discover an important lesson: little people are just no match for the 5-foot-3-inch or 6-foot-2-inch giants who set the rules. In essence, Rachel is learning about inadequacy — specifically, her own. Toddlers, even very smart, determined toddlers, cannot effectively impose their will upon that of a larger, stronger, and more experienced adult.

Coupled with the lesson on inadequacy is the uncomfortable feeling also associated with the earlier orange-juice-and-gravity experiment, *i.e.,* the pain of rejection. The adult whom the child depends upon for survival and love is not happy with the child. In fact, this adult is perceived as very upset and disapproving of the child. Face to face with adult demands and expectations, children quickly learn that certain consequences are associated with those demands. Many of the less-than-favorable responses involve rejection, and some may include physical punishment. The child concludes, "Not only are you unhappy with me because I didn't live up to your standards, but there is absolutely nothing I can do about it."

To be sure, children need limits. Healthy limits do not damage the child's sense of worth. Rather, the pain of rejection associated with "incorrect" behaviors, as determined by the limits, is what affects the child's feelings of worth. Because we're dealing with the human psyche and emotions, a number of linkages or associations are made. For example, the child's perception of its worth is not only associated with a threat to survival; it is now associated with not staying within the limits and obeying the rules. Rejection now means to the child that he or she is inadequate or incompetent — somehow incapable of conforming to acceptable standards for behavior.

When We Accede to Others' Demands

Perceived worth now becomes a matter of performing in line with adult demands and expectations. Feeling worthy is about conforming to certain expected standards. Failure to conform must mean the child is inadequate or incompetent, which in turn must mean he or she lacks worth. This experience is intensified because it is interpreted as a threat to survival and triggers the chemistry of the fight-or-flight response. In addition, a sense of injustice and lost innocence stirs feelings of guilt and hurt.

Such unfortunate lessons about inadequacy are provided at regular intervals throughout life. It happens to the elementary-school student who is always the last person chosen for a team in physical-education class. No one mistakes the message: "You're not very good, so we don't want you on our team." The lesson is clear for the middle-school or high-school student who is repeatedly teased about the way she dresses and is never asked out on a date. Rejections on college applications or job interviews provide additional lessons in inadequacy: "You just don't measure up." Whenever we put ourselves at risk of judgment by others and consequently experience rejection, it's pounded into us once again how inadequate we are.

And yet, is there anyone who is completely adequate for everything all the time? Is there anyone who is completely self-sufficient? Of course not! Self-sufficiency would suggest that you make your own clothes, you weave your own cloth, you build the car you drive to work every day, make every part, even drill for your own oil. You not only cook your own food — you grow it! Obviously no one is completely adequate for everything all the time. No one is completely self-sufficient. Even as adults, we are dependent on others for survival. Life intends us to be interdependent. We were not designed for solitude.

Put another way, we're all inadequate, every one of us. Even the most skilled, experienced person you know is inadequate in some way for something. Because everyone falls into this classification of inadequacy, this fact of life should be easy to accept; yet it's not. Inadequacy is difficult to accept and embrace because of our early indoctrination into the pain of rejection. The anger, fear, hurt, and guilt we felt and still feel when experiencing rejection for inadequacies causes us to work endlessly to become adequate — to be, or at least appear to be, perfect. We'll do almost anything to avoid the pain of rejection. And thus the games begin.

WORTH

REJECTION
Conditional
Worth

Anger – Fear
Guilt – Hurt

We experience rejection and the corresponding emotions as indicators of our inadequacy.

Inadequacy

INSIGHT QUESTIONS

Personal Growth:

• Think of a time when you felt inadequate. What were the circumstances? Who was involved? In what way did you or others see you as inadequate? What emotions were associated with the feeling of inadequacy?

Relationships:

• Have you ever made excuses to avoid being perceived as inadequate?

• In which relationships do you most often hide or attempt to conceal your inadequacies?

• Why is it so hard for us to admit and accept inadequacy?

Organizations:

• Are people in your organization encouraged to disclose their weaknesses as well as their strengths?

• How are areas of inadequacy dealt with in your company? What is the expectation regarding "adequate" performance?

6

The Mother of All Culture Games

Oh the games people play now,
Every night and every day now,
Never meaning what they say now,
Never saying what they mean.

— Joe South, "Games People Play"

Fashion trends are interesting. They're impossible to keep up with and often equally difficult to understand — especially the fashion trends of adolescents.

Justin had been out in the garage for a long time, rummaging around, obviously looking for something. Sitting at the table doing paperwork, his mother, Helen, hopelessly perplexed about what he could be doing out there, thought to herself, "I give up." "What are you doing out there?" she called, sticking her head out of the back door.

"I'm looking for something," the fourteen-year-old answered.

"Did you lose something?" she asked.

"No. I just need to find something."

"What?"

"A small chain," he answered.

"What do you need a chain for?" she inquired.

"For school."

"Are you working on a science project or something?" she ventured.

"No. I just need it for school. You wouldn't understand."

This was typical of many interactions lately: a lot of talk and very little real communication. So she closed the door and went back to her papers. "Oh, well, how much trouble can he get into in the garage?" she thought.

The purpose of the chain became apparent the next day. As Justin trotted to the car for his ride to school, Helen noticed something shiny dangling out from under his untucked shirt and swinging against his blue jeans down to the middle of his thigh. "What is that?" she inquired.

"It's a chain."

"What is it for?"

"It's like a wallet chain. You attach it to your wallet and hook the other end to your belt loop so no one can steal your wallet," he explained.

"Why are you taking your wallet to school?" she asked. "You don't need money at school."

"I'm not taking my wallet. Just the chain."

"I don't get it," Helen muttered.

"It's the style, Mom. C'mon, haven't you seen them? Everyone has them."

"Has someone been stealing wallets at your school?"

"No. It's not just about stealing. It's just cool. It's like construction workers wear them, so that when they're climbing on rafters and stuff, their wallet won't fall out and drop down underneath."

"According to my sources, you aren't exactly doing any construction work these days."

"It's cool, Mom. That's it," he snapped. "I just have to be careful that no one lifts my shirt or sees that I don't have a wallet attached. I've got to be careful to cover my pocket. That would be awful. You don't think they can see that, do you?"

Having an opportunity to provide welcome advice to her teenager was a rare event, so Helen dismissed the absurdity of the dangling chain and remarked, "It looks fine, honey. No one will notice."

Let the games begin! During adolescence the need to fit in and be popular is often of primary importance. Young people will do almost anything, sometimes engaging in dangerous acts, to feel a sense of belonging with others, to feel adequate, and to avoid rejection. While game playing may be particularly pronounced during the teenage years, it begins long before adolescence and continues long after.

Obviously, this is not a new idea. Eric Berne and Tom Harris popularized this observation in the 1960s through their books *Games People Play* and *I'm OK, You're OK*. Both authors described the various gaming techniques that occur in human relationships.

The reason we play such games is simple. It's because, by adulthood, we have all experienced our worth as conditional. We've had our inadequacies pointed out through rejection by others. This rejection was so painful and our reaction to it was so strong that we have learned to do almost anything to avoid feeling that pain again, to avoid being revealed as a "worthless" individual, plagued with faults. At least this is the dominant, although often unconscious, belief system.

So of course we play games. We take on roles. We pretend to be someone we're not, pretend to like things we don't, act interested when we're bored — anything to avoid revealing our shortcomings and being rejected. As soon as we accept the illusion that we are without worth unless we earn it, we enter into the "culture games." These are the games the child must master and sustain in order to avoid rejection. We learn these games by modeling the adults and peers in our environment, especially those we depend upon for love and support. Every one of us learns a variety of games designed to bring us recognition and self-esteem.

The Game of All Games

There are many different ways in which we hide our original or true selves, or otherwise play games with other people. In the end, it all can be reduced to the mother of all games: **Interact with people in such a way that what is unacceptable about yourself doesn't show.**

Succeeding at this game is very difficult, especially if we believe ourselves to be essentially without worth and continuously challenged to gain worth despite our many faults. Nevertheless, the game decrees that we must hide all our inadequacies — never let on that they exist. Ah, but this is only half of the story.

Like most children, when I was a child I enjoyed having friends over to play, at least most of the time. My mother had told me that a good host always allows the guest to choose which game will be played. Sometimes this meant that I was forced to play a game I didn't like, just because my friend chose it. I hated that rule, but I followed it. I followed it because it would prove that I was a "good host." The one thing I loved about the rule was it meant that when I was a guest at someone else's house, I could pick the game. It was automatic. No questions asked.

That is, until I visited Margaret. Every time I went to Margaret's house, she picked the game! I was terribly annoyed by this and one day decided to set her straight. "Margaret, don't you know anything?" I yelled. "A good host or hostess always lets the guest pick the game. What's wrong with you?" Well, that was the last time I played at Margaret's house. She stomped into the kitchen and ordered her mother to call my mother immediately. We were finished playing.

So now we get to the second half of the culture game: **Interact with people in such a way that what is unacceptable about yourself** *and the other person* **doesn't show.**

In other words, the basis for our culture games is hypocrisy. We play a series of games predicated on two-way hiding of what we think will elicit rejection of ourselves and what might bring about rejection of others from whom we want recognition and praise. I couldn't stay in relationship with Margaret so long as I was perfect and she was hopelessly flawed. Something was wrong with the game. I was only playing the first half of it. Both individuals need protection from disclosing their own inadequacies and having their inadequacies pointed out by the other, if the game is to have the desired result.

Worth vs. Self-Esteem

We now shift the discussion from a sense of worth to needs for recognition and self-esteem. There is a radical difference. We use the words self-concept, self-esteem, constructed self, and public self interchangeably. While they may vary slightly in definition, they are in essence the same. All these words refer to the self we create or construct to exhibit to others — the part of ourselves we allow others to see. These selves represent our efforts to receive recognition, praise, and love, or, at a minimum, avoid rejection. We construct these selves to regain *through others* a sense of our own original, unconditional worth.

Some may argue that a positive self-concept or sense of high self-esteem demonstrates an inner strength and is not created but rather expressed by an individual who recognizes and accepts his or her own talents. This commodity called self-esteem is viewed by society as desirable and healthy. Society assumes that those who are best at playing "chicken" are more valuable than those who have difficulty redirecting their need for creative transformation into the expected "pigeonholes." The child is taught to compare himself or herself with others and to compete for such things as grades in school, athletic prowess, artistic excellence, or anything else that allows one to excel and garner applause and praise. All of these efforts merely reinforce the culture games by establishing "chickenhood" as the desired goal and maintaining that worth is gained through performance.

Certainly, many people take pride in their talents and skills. Even so, we discover the value of these talents and skills because of the recognition and praise we receive from others. Although as an adult I may have internalized my own value for my special talents, I was first taught to value my talents because others valued them. And if suddenly everyone else found the expression of my talent distasteful or otherwise abnormal, I would probably experience the pain of rejection and likely abandon my gift.

For this reason, the pursuit of self-esteem and a positive self-image, as *popularly known,* moves us further away from our original and true creative selves and closer to a constructed self that we believe to be acceptable by society. We undertake to construct a self-concept in order to develop a self that can interact with others in such a way that what is unacceptable about oneself and others doesn't show. It's the same old game! The self-concept is a constructed self designed to hide what we fear will bring rejection. In essence, there are now two selves: the private, creative self (designed to engage in transforming creativity) and the public, conditioned self (in which innate creativity is channeled toward fitting into the pecking order of "chickenhood"). One can see this dual reality beginning to form at a very young age.

My mother lived on a very busy and narrow street. There was lots of traffic, and it all moved fast. Whenever I took my children for a visit, they were told not to get too close to the street. More specifically, they were not to get close to the mailbox — that was too far.

One day my oldest decided to do Grandma a favor and fetch the mail. She believed she was old enough to watch for the traffic and carefully extracted the mail from the box. With good intentions at heart and mail in hand, she headed back for the house and was promptly met by her very angry grandmother shaking her finger frantically and shouting, "You know better, young lady! How many times have I told you not to do that! What on earth were you thinking?" Grandma's face was fierce and clearly disapproving. Feeling the blow of the words, the little girl looked up, angry and hurt, and said, "You can make us do what you want, but you don't know what we're thinking."

You have to love the kid! Forced into compliance, like all children, she was still maintaining a private identity that was hers and hers alone. Yes, she would conform to the rules and regulations, even when she didn't want to, or disagreed. On the outside, she would do all the right things. On the inside, she would have her own thoughts, opinions, and dreams — not to be shared with others.

Ego: Weakness or Strength?

The creative self, based on worth, is hidden beneath the constructed self, which is rooted in the fear of rejection. This social constructed self is popularly referred to as the ego. It is important to note that ego, understood in this sense, is built on fear. Sometimes in advance of working with a particular group of people we are told, "Be forewarned. There are a lot of strong egos in this group." The implication is that strong egos mean strong individuals.

Unfortunately, the opposite is true. The more insecure and fearful we become, the stronger the "ego" or persona we require in order to hide our fear. This is why so many people we identify as having "big egos" compulsively strive to be at the top of the pecking order. They need to be seen at the top, in order to mask their own insecurities. Therefore, in a group of "strong egos," we can assume there are a lot of scared people.

At the deepest level, we fear that our own creative self will escape from the limited box of the "ego" or constructed self and soar toward the cloudless sky of creative transformation. We have learned to fear being our authentic or original selves. The constructed self-concept is based on what others and we think we ought to be, not on who we really are. Instead of being ourselves, we choose, with the questionably helpful reinforcement of others, to be someone else.

Our creative self is buried beneath the game structures we build up in order to avoid rejection and the pain of not being seen to have worth. Hence the illusion of lack of worth has evolved into a belief that we must be someone other than who we are. We must continue to cluck, scratch, and fly a few feet in the air and avoid thoughts of soaring majestically, high above the barnyard. We have become so afraid of who we really are that we require constant reassurance that we are conforming and performing well as the someone we're not.

Longings That Are Never Satisfied

This striving for continual affirmation is often experienced as a longing, an emptiness, a hungering, a thirsting, or a restlessness that we can't quite put a finger on. Because construction of the self-concept suppresses the creative self, we experience an emerging loneliness and vague sense of isolation even when we are with others. Solitude and silence become threatening because the constructed self needs continuous reminding of its value, and we have set ourselves up to garner that from everyone else. Although we're told, "It's better to be alone than in bad company," many of us, especially the young, will choose any company, good or bad, to avoid being alone. Games only work when there are others around to help us play them — to provide the recognition we need for our successes. On the other hand, a compulsive need for successes makes the threat of failure even more frightening.

What we have described is the descent of the mind into illusion and destructive game playing. As Dr. Erle Fitz states, "The inauthentic has become the model of what ought to be." Building our lives on an illusion is like building a house on sand. It is not a solid or substantial foundation. It leaves us vulnerable to the emotional storms of rejection and requires a life of evasion.

WORTH

REJECTION
Conditional
Worth

**Anger – Fear
Guilt – Hurt**

Through game-playing, we become masters of deception in the effort to mask our inadequacies and those of others.

Inadequacy

**Culture
Game**

INSIGHT QUESTIONS

Personal Growth:

- Ideal images take many forms. They can include ideals for where you live, what kind of job you have, how you look, how your children behave, etc. Do an honest assessment of yourself. How important is it to you to fit a certain image? If not, do you have an equally strong need NOT to fit it? (This is also an image requirement.)

Relationships:

- How important is it for you to "fit in" with a certain group? What kind of effort does it take on your part to be accepted?

- How do you feel about people who work at being accepted? Do such people become unacceptable in your opinion? Are you more accepting of people who aren't making an effort to be accepted?

Organizations:

- What expectations regarding image exist in your organization? Do you ever feel pressured to fit a certain standard? Is that standard related to effective job performance?

- How does your organization handle people who don't "fit in"?

7

The Ego Has Landed

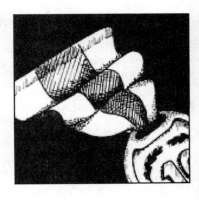

"Too many people overvalue what they are not and undervalue what they are."

— Malcolm Forbes

Frank was a young man with a plan. He was a teenager driven by hormones (and his parents' old station wagon — at least they agreed he could borrow it on Saturday night). Frank was in search of the perfect girl, the "all-American" girl who would agree to accompany him on a date.

Throughout every day, Frank carried on a process of elimination. He evaluated each member of the opposite sex whom he saw or talked with. Did she meet the requirements for the "all-American" girl? This was a critical question, because Frank saw himself as the all-American guy. So, finding the perfect date was important.

Now, don't get the wrong idea about Frank. He's not conceited nor terribly picky or judgmental about others. Like most people, Frank has merely fallen prey to a lifetime of suggestions about what it means to be cool, strong, handsome, smart, etc. He works very hard to ensure that he is the perfect picture of all these things. And of course, he wants the companion on his arm to meet his ideal notions about beauty, sensitivity, friendliness, intelligence, and so on. So his search began.

After several years of trial and error, in which a number of young ladies have fallen hopelessly short of his ideal and for one reason or another failed to see Frank as the ideal specimen he considers himself to be, Frank finally discovers one young lady who seems nearly perfect. As he gets to know her better, *he concludes that this particular young lady seems very close to his ideal female. And, as luck would have it, she thinks that Frank is very nearly the ideal male. Obviously, Frank was a pretty good judge when he chose her.*

On this note, Frank and his female friend decide to make a permanent habit of their togetherness by getting married. Everything runs smoothly until shortly after the honeymoon, when normal day-to-day routines set in. At this point, things begin to change. Although neither was aware of it before, both are now crystal-clear about not only the all-American male and female, but also the ideal husband and the ideal wife. And each partner thinks the other is poorly informed about the matter. Frank very quickly ascertains that his partner is terribly misinformed about what it means to be the ideal wife. Her comments also suggest that she has some mistaken notions about what the ideal husband is supposed to do and be. In the early stages of beginning to clean up one another's act, Frank and his bride discover they will soon be parents.

Not long after the arrival of the baby two additional roles are layered on — the ideal mother and the ideal father — to co-mingle with the all-American male and female and the ideal husband and wife. Now things get really complicated. Frank has always been very clear about what it means to be the all-American male and the all-American female, the ideal husband and the ideal wife, and the perfect father and the perfect mother. His wife also has very clear images of each of these six roles firmly rooted in her own mind. Now 12 different roles collide as the couple tries to work together to raise their child. It sometimes seems that an entire army of people, including all the in-laws and experienced friends who ever influenced Frank and his wife, have arrived on the scene with the best and the latest parenting and marital advice!

The only thing left to determine is how much money to save for the child's inevitable psychotherapy bills!

Remember the old comic advertisement depicting a big tough bully on the beach kicking sand in the face of the 97-pound weakling? The muscular hunk, despite his rude behavior, represented the ideal.

Not only was it important to be like him, it was unacceptable to be the little weak guy in the ad. So you bought the product — a muscle-building device (and numerous products since then) — to increase the odds of achieving the ideal.

Not unlike the teenager with the new fashion requirement, Frank and his wife have discovered that ideal roles and images are in actuality demands and expectations. Frank has built up a very clear image of the all-American female, the ideal wife, and the perfect mother. He also expects that the person he chooses will agree with his criteria (although they were never discussed in any depth) and perform accordingly. When this fails to happen, Frank's ideal images are disrupted, and what was once an expectation evolves into demands for his wife's behavior, appearance, and ways of thinking. Of course, Frank's wife has her own ideal images, expectations, and demands for Frank's performance. Both partners will inevitably fall short of the other's demands in some way or another.

We find it easy to relate Frank's story to someone else, more difficult to recognize him in ourselves. Nevertheless, most of us can understand this story. Think about what it's like when you're dating or just getting to know someone for the first time. It's highly improbable that any one of us ever began a new relationship by stating, "Uh . . . listen . . . before we go any further . . . let me share a few things about myself. You see, I have this mole . . . and, well . . . it's in a peculiar place. And I have an uncanny ability to develop morning breath at any hour of the day or night." Or, "Before we get to know each other better, I really must tell you that, well, uh, I have some pretty atrocious bathroom habits." No, we've never begun a relationship this way either!

Such an introduction, however honest, is not considered the "normal" or acceptable way of beginning a relationship. Our culture game dictates that we interact with others in such a way that what is unacceptable about the other person and ourselves does not show. So, it's a rare person who begins a conversation in this atypical, off-putting fashion. If you've ever been on the receiving end of such a comment, you remember that you probably very quickly excused yourself from the scene.

For Frank and his wife (and others like them), the tension builds over time. With mounting frustration, both partners find it progressively more difficult to fit the demands and expectations of the other and go on concealing what is perceived as unacceptable about either one. Each person must expend more energy to sustain the relationship within tolerable limits. In many marriages, conversations eventually must be limited to certain topics to avoid explosive arguments. These relationships are like walking through a minefield. If he brings up one subject, she blows up. If she brings up another subject, he blows up, and in certain subject areas, such as finances, they both blow up. In order to have any peace and quiet at all, only a few, safe topics for conversation can be pursued. The end result? Superficiality, absence of intimacy, and boredom. Unfortunately, this dynamic applies in relationships of many types; it is by no means restricted to marriage.

Images and Roles

What happened to Frank and his wife in the story happens to all of us, to varying degrees. We are taught, through everyday socialization processes and conditioning, to value certain behaviors or images to the exclusion of others. This is how an eagle learns to value scratching, clucking, and flying a few feet more than soaring majestically through the sky. The bottom line remains the same: roles and images enable us to play the culture game successfully, then solidify over time into demands for ourselves and for others. Examples of ideal behavior are rigidified and now must be lived up to. The rules must be strictly adhered to if we are to sustain the insatiable quest to feel worthy. Violation of the rules ends in rejection and a perceived loss of worth.

People create demands and expectations around myriad images and roles. Consider all the things you do in your life — the various roles you play. Perhaps you are an employee, a manager, a member of a civic group or a church, an athlete or coach, an artist or hobbyist. You're also a child, you may be a sibling, and you're a friend, possibly a spouse, perhaps a parent. The potential list is endless. Now, roles are not inherently bad. In fact, roles help us to organize our lives. They help us focus energy on certain people or certain tasks, depending on the situation.

The danger in the roles we play lies in our learned propensity to ignore who we really are, in our cultivated suppression of our original, creative selves. This happens when a subordinate tells her boss what she thinks the boss wants to hear. It happens when a manager says what she thinks a "good manager" would say. It happens again when a parent says what he believes a "good parent" is supposed to say when telephoned by the school principal. It happens when we lie to those close to us because we're afraid to speak the truth.

As images and roles solidify into demands and expectations, we find ourselves plagued by questions. Do our peers perceive us as good co-workers? Are we getting regular pay increases, bonuses, and promotions? Are we being good neighbors? Is the lawn mowed, the house painted, the car new enough, and are we dressed for success? Are we on the right boards and committees, members of politically and socially correct clubs and organizations? Are our kids bringing home the right grades, winning at sports, or taking honors in the art competition? An endless list of achievements or affiliations becomes the basis for building or losing self-esteem — for perceived success or failure.

Summing it up, roles are fine to help organize our lives. Roles and images become detrimental when they replace unique personalities and authentic, creative selves. Roles are destructive when they lead to inflated self-esteem or an overbearing ego, when the smallest of slips destroys one's sense of worth.

Roles lose their utility when we lose sight of the person beneath all the various roles we play, when we forget what we really want, when we choose not to communicate to others our real dreams, fears, ideas, and questions. The loneliness of the creative self is the result. Demands and expectations put in place to attain and maintain worth by proving to others that we are a good this or a good that cause us to lose sight of ourselves. We become strangers to our original, creative selves. We don't know why we feel confused, where the anxiety or uneasiness is coming from, why we're just not satisfied, why we feel angry and suspicious of others. We don't know because we don't know who we really are.

Control, Certainty, Stability, Security

Life in "chickenhood" becomes an endless struggle to keep everything intact. This struggle takes on various forms. For some of us, it is a continual effort to maintain control. For others, it's an overwhelming need for certainty. For others, only a solid sense of stability or security will satisfy. And yet none of these goals is wholly achievable. The smallest change can quickly disrupt our comfort level or equilibrium. Why? Because each of these things — control, certainty, stability, and security — is an illusion. When have we ever been in complete control of our lives and the world around us? When is anything ever certain? What is stability in an ever-changing world? When does one ever feel completely secure and invulnerable?

To the constructed self, the opposite approach to striving for these illusions is frightening. The opposite approach to control is surrender. Instead of certainty, accepting unpredictability and probability. Instead of stability and the status quo, being open to change and the unknown. Rather than the unending quest for assurance and security, becoming willing to risk and act from faith. For the constructed self, who has learned to believe that such a position places one's worth on the line, the risk seems too great.

At this point, the journey is complete. The false ego has landed. The trust of the child has given way to a demand for security. The child's curiosity is buried by the need for certainty. Creativity has been stifled by the need for stability. Unconditional worth is no longer unconditional. Worth must now be earned, and efforts and images must be managed, to meet our assumed demands for others and ourselves.

WORTH

REJECTION
Conditional
Worth

Anger – Fear
Guilt – Hurt

Inadequacy

Culture games are solidified into performance demands for ourselves and others. These demands define our false self or ego.

Demand

Culture Game

INSIGHT QUESTIONS

Personal Growth:

• What are some of the roles and images you feel obligated to maintain?

• How do you feel when your performance doesn't live up to your standards?

Relationships:

• How do you feel when others suggest that you have let them down?

• How do these feelings trigger your own sense of inadequacy and affect your own expectations for yourself?

Organizations:

• Which of the illusions do you favor — certainty, stability, security, or control?

• How does your organization seek to maintain these illusions?

8

The Origin of Stress

"Discouragement is simply the despair of wounded self-love."
— François de Fénélon

Patrick is the software design group vice-president for one of the top five high-tech companies in the world. And he's excited. No, he's beyond excited. Patrick is ecstatic, because he and his colleagues have secured an unprecedented partnership with a competitor to design and introduce unique new software. Not only is the idea of this new product a breakthrough, but a cooperative relationship with a top competitor is unheard of in the history of his company. Patrick and his colleagues have set a new standard.

Patrick spent the past month on a whirlwind tour where he presented this new strategy to his own top management, successfully convincing them of its merit; to other divisions within his company, who listened with amazement; and to several divisions within the partnering company. Enthusiasm swelled, and all eyes were on Patrick and his design team to complete the first leg of the project within six months — approximately one-third of the typical design time.

Now, the day has finally arrived for Patrick to make the final announcement of the project, the overall strategy, the partnership, and the timelines to his own team. Of course, he has spoken with a number of individuals at various times about what is possible, but no one is truly aware of the whole picture and how it has finally developed. This is a proud moment for Patrick, for he knows that the real work is about to begin. He depends on this design team for success, and *he can't wait to hear their response.*

Patrick has scheduled this meeting at an off-site conference center. He's ordered several dozen helium balloons to be released at just the right moment, and a fully stocked ice-cream sundae bar for the indulgence of all present. This will be a celebration! He will make the presentation, answer any questions, and then the party will begin!

Patrick is pleased with the turnout, especially in light of the hectic work schedules. Everyone knows this is an important meeting. Everything starts off as planned. The balloons are released on cue. But nothing has prepared Patrick for the reaction his presentation receives.

As Patrick finishes and opens the floor for questions, he looks out upon a sea of blank stares. There are no questions, no comments. People sit motionless in their chairs. There is no excitement. There is no response.

"What's wrong with you guys?" he asks. "Is it confusing? Did I fail to make something clear? What don't you understand in all this?"

With still no response, Patrick assumes he missed a major point, goes back to his overhead transparencies, and quickly walks through his entire presentation again. Throughout his effort, he looks desperately toward his audience for the support and enthusiasm he believes they should feel. But what he expects is simply not there.

"Don't you all have anything to say? What's wrong with you? I don't understand this response."

As the group remains motionless and silent, Patrick raises his voice. "Everywhere I've been, I've received nothing but excitement, enthusiasm, and sometimes even amazement! Now, when I bring this back to you, I get nothing: a bunch of blank faces! You'd think I just told you someone died! What's wrong with you? Don't you get it! Where's your excitement?"

The response: nothing.

Patrick's frustration is evident. This is what happens when demands are left unfulfilled. Evidently, Patrick has some demands as to how his team should respond. When their behavior doesn't match his demands, things start to heat up.

The Chicken Conspiracy

What Patrick doesn't understand is that he has just disrupted all perceptions of control, certainty, stability, and security previously held by the members of this team. Patrick's remarks have just been heard by his team this way: "We are about to make something that has never been made before. No one knows how to do it, and it must be complete within unheard-of time constraints. The success of this effort, our partnership with a competitor, my job and yours depend on your finding the solution. And, by the way, I know you will." In this context, the deadening silence is more easily understood.

Patrick has unknowingly triggered a sense of inadequacy in his listeners. To a certain extent, this may have been unavoidable. "You're asking me to do something that I'm not sure I can do," could have been the response. "In addition, you're saying that the success of the project and my worth as an engineer are on the line." The conditionality of worth is rarely clearer.

Possibly there were other interpretations in the room that day. Nevertheless, that was the primary reaction, leaving the group needing to let things "soak in" before asking questions, offering comments, or otherwise expressing excitement or dread. In truth, Patrick was addressing a group that included some remarkable people. Some held patents on inventions — natural problem solvers who got their biggest "high" solving a problem no one else could solve. They had faced this situation before — never with such short timelines — but otherwise this was familiar territory. Any who responded in this way would adjust and begin to see the challenge as an opportunity to do the impossible, their associated anxiety eventually serving as fuel for innovation.

Others, however, had a competing demand or expectation that was equally valid. They wanted everything they produced to be of the highest quality, and they were convinced that no one could design, test, and introduce such a product in six months and still meet standards for quality. This response poses an interesting dilemma, one that is not easily resolved. The demands and expectations of this group were in direct conflict with Patrick's. He wanted enthusiasm, while they refused to get excited about anything that might turn out to be inferior. Who will win?

This is an important question in light of the culture game. Remember, the culture game dictates that we interact with others in such a way that what is inadequate or unacceptable about others and

66

ourselves does not show. However, it is not always possible even within the confines of this game to enable everyone to look good — to appear flawless — all the time. This particularly holds true when we have competing goals. When demands are in direct competition, the perception is that someone will win and someone will lose. **The popular notion of a "both/and" or a "win/win" only works when both parties are willing to let go of their separate demands and expectations enough to make room for those of the other person.** For the majority of people, a perceived challenge to worth will only cause us to have greater conviction for our demands: we lock in. Again, someone will win, maintain self-esteem, and appear successful, and someone else will lose, sacrifice self-esteem, and be branded the loser.

How Loved Ones Fit Into the Game

When we find that our demands clash with those of someone we love, we tend to work even harder to keep the culture game intact. This skewed belief system argues that I must save face in order to secure your love and acceptance, and because of the feelings I have for you, I will work harder to help you save face. But, finally, if the struggle persists, the drive to preserve self will override the drive to protect another.

This whole set-up makes people sound a bit uncivilized. It's not at all the way we like to think about ourselves or our fellow human beings. Nevertheless, when we believe that worth is on the line, and the tightly woven net of the constructed self or ego begins to disintegrate in frustration, then stress arises, and our least attractive behaviors surface. When my unconditional worth as a creative person is perceived no longer as a given, but rather as a commodity to be earned, demands skyrocket, and opportunities for frustration abound.

We All Express Emotions Differently

Patrick had a particular expectation for his team that seemed harmless enough. He wanted them to be excited, to be enthusiastic. Nothing wrong with that. The problem arose because Patrick is very clear about how being excited and enthusiastic looks and feels to him, and he has demanded that everyone else demonstrate these feelings in the same way. It's interesting to see how far we take our demands and expectations. Patrick not only expected the team to be excited, he also expected them to demonstrate their excitement immediately in the same fashion he would. His inability to detect excitement as he defines it within his time frame does not mean that no one was excited. They all were responding in their different ways. For some in the group, excitement might have been more clearly observable if Patrick could have seen the inner workings of their brains. Inside their heads, the "cogs" and "switches" were humming as they immediately went to work on the problem. While they appeared apathetic, anxious, or concerned on the outside, they were already beginning to tackle the problem on the inside.

With such plentiful demands applying to virtually every situation and relationship, you or I may gain or lose face in the eyes of others in any social situation. Hence most of us are forever on guard to control any given situation, so that our demands will be fulfilled and we gain recognition and esteem, while evading the hurt of failure and rejection. Every situation becomes a two-edged sword. We can succeed or fail in any situation, and to the extent that we've accepted the illusion that worth is conditional and must be proven or earned, every situation is an opportunity to risk our worth.

Take a moment to think about life in the emerging global information age. How many times per day do we put ourselves or allow others to put us into situations of success or failure? How many deadlines are piling up where we can be late and thereby "prove" our inadequacy? How many things do we say "yes" to when we need to be saying "no"? How many things are number-one priorities? How many of us are, to varying degrees, stressed out?

The Origin of Stress

Stress is the hallmark response to the pursuit of worth as the reward for success. The illusion that worth is conditional on performance, achievement, or recognition, bases worth on living up to demands and expectations constructed by ourselves and others. Yet, personal worth is not an illusion — it is a given. And in our efforts to regain what we never lost, we become progressively self-conscious, overloaded, and exhausted. We become preoccupied with meeting our own and others' demands and expectations. We become obsessed by the quest to satisfy our demands for security, stability, certainty, and control. When our demands or others' are disrupted, we experience stress. The stress we experience is our emotional response to actual or feared loss of control, security, certainty, or stability.

In an effort to regain control, security, certainty, and stability, we attempt to force ourselves and others to align with our demands. Maintaining the culture game requires tremendous effort. The need for control, security, certainty, and stability is fear-based. This need is rooted in the dynamic of the constructed self operating out of fear of loss of worth, rather than in the creative self operating from an acceptance of worth. Once we allow our original self to become buried beneath the culture game's layers of images, roles, demands, and expectations, we begin mistaking our controlling constructed self for who we really are. We have *become* someone other than who we really are. This is how the eagle, surrounded by the barnyard environment of the chicken, accepts himself as a chicken and disregards the eagle within. Our illusion becomes our reality. The stress that results from constantly struggling to meet increasing demands is the price we pay for disguising and burying our unique, original, and creative selves.

Being Our True Selves

This illusion might be seen as a form of waking sleep, or collective hypnosis. We are dreaming that we are someone we aren't. We are eagles dreaming that we are chickens. We have given up expecting that we can fly more than a few feet in the air, yet there is an unfulfilled longing to do so. Because it is an illusion, it must constantly be recreated and reinforced. We need continuous affirmation to keep the illusion going. We strive ceaselessly to be the best cluckers and scratchers in the barnyard, sustaining the effort primarily by internal self-talk and the assurance from others that this is who we are.

Have you ever heard someone say, "You're not yourself today"? What they mean is that you are not behaving in your habitual way. For those of us still trapped in chickenhood, our habitual selves are our conventional, constructed, conforming selves. Perhaps the best response may be "No, I haven't been myself for a long time. And I've decided it's time to start."

WORTH

REJECTION
Conditional
Worth

**Anger – Fear
Guilt – Hurt**

*We experience
frustration and stress
when our demands
on others and
ourselves are not
met.*

Frustration

Inadequacy

Demand

**Culture
Game**

INSIGHT QUESTIONS

Personal Growth:

- How do you handle surprises? Do you like surprises, or do you prefer predictability, certainty, stability, or control?

- Do you have a pet peeve? What is it? What do you feel and do when someone displays your pet peeve? Do you think this observation can teach you anything about yourself?

Relationships:

- Think about some of your closest personal and work relationships. What behaviors on the part of others really frustrate you and generate stress?

- In these instances, how are your demands and expectations in competition with the demands and expectations of others?

Organizations:

- Consider the following statement: "You can expect people to do what they do."

- Has your organization ever asked you to think "outside the box" and be creative? What has been the response to those who have?

- If people in your organization "do what they do," why do you expect them to do anything different? How is frustration generated within your organization when people "do what they do"?

9

The Vicious Circle

*"You have no idea what a poor opinion I have of myself
— and how little I deserve it."*

— W. S. Gilbert

I met David a few years ago while conducting a seminar
on personal mastery. David is an extremely successful entre-
preneur. Years ago, he purchased a wire and cable manufac-
turing company out of bankruptcy, using a relatively small
inheritance. At the time, he considered the purchase his one
chance to "make it big." And he made it. David is now a multi-
millionaire, envied by most everyone who knows him.

The seminar wasn't designed for a typical business group.
It was a five-day gathering held off-site in a lovely wooded
area. The participants came from all walks of life, including a
housewife, a clergyman, an educator, a politician, a physician,
and several business people. Considering David's background,
I was a bit surprised to see him in the course. Nevertheless,
I found him to be outgoing, friendly, and very likable — not
to mention impressive. David was certainly the only one who
arrived in his own private plane!

Well into the third day of the seminar, the other participants began to lose patience with David's behavior. Others
participated in many moments of self-disclosure, yet David
had spoken very little. He appeared to be just listening and
reflecting. His lack of participation bothered several people,
and one person began to probe to find out why he remained
so quiet in the sessions while being so warm and outgoing at
meals and during free time.

The Vicious Circle

David's expression changed dramatically upon being questioned. He looked ill and hesitated before saying that it was hard for him to share his personal side. Even so, David began talking about his business career and many successes. He told about exotic trips to the Orient, safaris in Africa, and visits to places most of us had only read about. He reported that he was building a second house for his wife in Florida. He spoke of his many acquisitions: a yacht, plane, and numerous automobiles.

In the midst of telling his story, David lurched forward, clutched at his stomach, and began to sob. We were all startled. After a few moments, he went into greater depth with his report. He was building the second house to try to win his wife back, for she had given up on a real relationship with him and had left him. All of the adult toys that he believed marked his success were insufficient to attract regular visits from his now grown children, whom he hardly knew. In fact, David was miserable. He had recently lost two-thirds of his stomach to the surgeon's knife, and he had no one to turn to for love and support. David concluded his sad story thus: "I've gained the whole world and lost everything that's really important to me."

The group then learned that David was a compulsive worker. He had made it to the top of his business game, yet he was confused, uncertain of his true identity, and knew that the price he had paid was too high. He had done what he thought was right, playing the game to the finish. He had been the determined competitor, yet now he was lonely and depressed.

Beneath the outgoing, hard-hitting business façade was a gentle person —a person who, out of fear, had competed with the best. It was only now, bent over in tears and pain, that he was learning who he really was beneath the forged exterior. Somehow, somewhere, he had bought into the notion that his gentleness was a handicap. He stated his long-held belief: "Either you are a strong and tough competitor, or you're a wimp." He had no model for being both strong and gentle, no notion that both were possible in the same person.

David's story was and is all too familiar. In his case, the images, roles, and games of the constructed false self were rapidly falling apart. Although largely unaware of it, David had suppressed any inclinations that did not fit into his image of being macho and successful. Many of his valuable original characteristics were buried, because he judged them inadequate and unacceptable. He was afraid to be himself, his real and genuine self. His original, creative self was a stranger to his false, constructed self. And yet from society's point of view he was normal. He was doing what many successful people are supposed to do. Unfortunately, being "normal" seldom means being our true selves.

In the 1940s there was a radio game show called "Truth or Consequences." Its name suggests the implications of trying to live out the illusion of being someone other than who you are. In many ways, David had denied his *truth,* and he is now painfully aware of his *consequences.* His tears and painful deformed stomach were a testimonial to his gamble to be someone he wasn't. The party was over, and he knew it. Culture reinforces us in a multitude of ways to become someone we're not. Not unlike a social hypnosis or collective sleep, the more we identify with the illusion the more we become a stranger to our creative self. We live the illusion as if it were the only reality.

Images of Unreality

Consider society's methods. Commercial advertising is a prime example. Young people who have never been overweight pose for ads to entice the obese to become slim and trim. Myriad creams, ointments, oils, and soaps promise a return of youth, reduced cellulite, and prevention of aging in the quest to look 10 to 20 years younger than we really are. The next time you're standing in a line at the grocery store, examine the popular magazines for women. Eighty percent of them in any given month will couple pictures of sumptuous desserts with headlines for rapid weight loss! Every imaginable type of exercise equipment is on the market for bulging biceps, washboard abs, thin thighs, and reshaping of every other part of our anatomies to conform to some ideal physique. Of course, it's not the exercise that's negative. Exercise can be desirable and lead to better health. The illusion takes over when we work out compulsively every day to attain and maintain some ideal image, rather than simply for the pleasure and benefits of good health and fitness.

Television advertising's effort to reinforce the illusion is echoed by the programs themselves. Soap operas are perhaps the most insidious. These ongoing sagas condition and reinforce an enormous number of social games, roles, and images for those who watch them. Popular novels, tabloid newspapers, and the lyrics of much of our music also portray the games and images as real life — as if there were no alternative. The assumption seems to be that if enough people believe it, it must be true. Even though almost everyone used to believe the world was flat, believing didn't make it so.

Impossibility Leads to Distress

In the end, trying to be who we aren't and evading who we are is a constant struggle. Trying to meet all our own and others' demands and expectations comes with a very high price tag — predictable and often painful consequences. Attempting to maintain the various cultural roles and games while attempting to achieve our ideal images of attractiveness, intelligence, talent, superiority, compassion, efficiency, effectiveness, and all-around top performance adds up to an impossible task.

With the possibility of failure, the fear of exposing our inadequacies takes hold and reactivates the fight-or-flight process. We can fight to regain control in order to evade the fear and hurt of being inadequate and unacceptable, or else we can simply retreat into aggressive passivity. For adults, however, the process becomes far more than a simple case of fight-or-flight. Instead of activating the process designed to preserve life, we have somehow transformed it into life-threatening stress.

What was once the chemistry of survival is now the chemistry of stress. The very process that, at the biological level, serves the survival drive, becomes a trigger for many of our symptoms and diseases. The anger is no longer simple anger; in the adolescent and adult it may take the form of hostility. Many depressed men and women are, at root, people who have not been given permission, or have not given themselves permission, to feel or express their deep-seated anger. Fight is no longer reserved for protecting one's life but now takes the form of belittling others and putting them down.

Even without a physical threat, someone who feels psychologically and emotionally hurt tries to hurt back, in some cases lashing out at anyone who happens to be available. When the hostility is directed at you, it is difficult to remember that a hostile person is a hurting person. Something is wrong. They are hurting and fearful, and because they can't make the pain go away, they try to pass on that hurt to someone else. Of course this doesn't make perfect logical sense, and the dynamic is most often unconscious to the attacker.

In adults, the simple fear of the fight-or-flight process becomes anxiety. In simple fear, there is actual threat to personal survival. When a poisonous snake is turned loose, fear is a normal and appropriate reaction, because one's life is at risk. When adults become anxious over their potential failure, they are seldom in any real physical danger, although they respond emotionally as if they were. When you or I experience anxiety, we may, typically, be unclear about the nature of the danger we face. Instead, we feel a general sense of frustration, inadequacy, and helplessness to avoid an anticipated failure.

Just as anger and fear are transformed into hostility and anxiety in the adult, so guilt and hurt are transformed into shame and blame. When the guilt and hurt are turned inward, the person experiences shame. When they are turned outward, the person projects blame. Scapegoating others is a perfect example. Persons riddled with anxiety feel shameful for their condition and blame others for their lot. Hostile people blame others as well and feel shame in the aftermath of their own rage.

Guilt and its derivatives are perhaps the most complex aspects of the stress process. Authentic guilt emerges when we recognize our own hypocrisy in denying our true self in the effort to be someone we're not. This form of guilt can be an important wake-up call to living more fully from our creative self. Within the illusory game-playing world of ideal images and roles, another form of guilt occurs when our demands are frustrated, that is, when we or others fail to "measure up." This is inauthentic or enculturated guilt. It is inauthentic because the frustrated demands and expectations were designed to help us be someone we're not! Until I understand the process, I feel guilty when I fail to master my demands and fulfill my expectations, which were designed to construct the person I think I want to be. All the while I hide away my original, creative self for fear of rejection. While this contortion can seem humorous to an onlooker, it is deadly serious when you're caught in it.

The Vicious Circle

Surely it's only we human beings who can create such a curious set of experiences. Consider the following logic spiral. When an adult's demands are disrupted, frustration sets in. If the demands are important enough, or if such disruption occurs repeatedly, stress erupts, and the adult fight-or-flight emotions of anxiety, hostility, shame, and blame are triggered. Once caught in this negativity, the adult begins to reject herself and her own behavior. Because such rejection is in direct violation of her sense of worth, the cycle begins again of conditional worth, striving to overcome inadequacy, gaming, demands and expectations, frustration, and stress. This is the vicious circle. And unfortunately, we are all caught in it to varying degrees at various times in our lives.

Emotions Serve a Purpose

The basic emotions of anger, fear, guilt, and hurt are not innately bad. Nor are they only a part of the constructed self. Human beings were designed from birth to experience a wide array of emotions; these four emotions are part of the total repertoire. In this sense, anger, fear, guilt, and hurt are a part of the creative self. In fact, these are the emotions we feel when we are not acting in accordance with our creative self. The emotions serve as an alerting process to let us know when we're getting off track, or to let us know that another's behavior may be violating our own or someone else's inherent worth. These emotions can lead us back to being our true, original, creative selves.

Hurt warns us when we are denying our capacity to experience transforming creativity. Hurt is also the basis for human compassion. When we are not acting out of integrity, guilt reminds us that we can do better at being authentic. Fear warns us of impending life-threatening situations, and anger helps us to protect ourselves against threats and provides energy to fight for justice. In their original forms, these emotions are life-giving and life-saving. Once these emotions move through the culture game, however, they work against us and become destructive. We use the hurt to hurt others and ourselves. Our guilt becomes enculturated, turns against us, and we become crippled and immobilized — afraid to be real. The anger is turned into life-threatening hostility, and we are terrorized when fear becomes the anxiety of failure.

These emotions only become destructive when translated through the adult's constructed self or false ego. The adult version of hostility, anxiety, shame, and blame dissipates energy and undermines the body's immune system, making us more susceptible to accidents and more vulnerable to disease. What tended to be constructive in the young becomes destructive in the adult. Frustrated demands and expectations generate stress. Prolonged stress is the precursor of a wide variety of symptoms.

Biology and Feelings

Earlier we observed that when a child is angry or fearful, he or she is angry or fearful all over. The biochemistry seeks expression, and for the child it is discharged through shouting, crying, hitting, kicking, running, throwing, and various other tantrum-like behaviors. Adults, on the other hand, like to believe they're more civilized and hence avoid behaving in this way. Think about your own response when your boss or some other authority figure criticizes you. If he or she is really letting you have it, you may feel emotions ranging from embarrassment to rage, but rather than let your boss know, you quietly squelch your anger or hurt and save it for some poor unsuspecting soul you encounter later — or perhaps your dog. Maybe you are in such control that no one knows you were just devastated. Yet, if we don't deal with our feelings, our feelings will deal with us.

So, what happens to all those chemicals — the chemistry of stress? They have to go somewhere, and an adult who "has it all together" rarely, if ever, directly lets them out. Many times the chemistry is discharged in the direction of a spouse or a child, while driving (road rage), through hobbies or exercise, or managed, for some, by self-medication with alcohol or other drugs. Regardless of the target, the chemistry must go somewhere, and adults are notorious for repressing and storing up these emotions until they explode. When the chemistry is not directly discharged, it is released through other systems of the body that were not intended for such expression, and it can then trigger a host of stress-related illnesses. The end result of prolonged stress is a predictable spectrum of psychophysiological symptoms, occurring as the unacknowledged, unexpressed emotions of the creative self are diverted into the service of the constructed self.

Loneliness is one of the most commonly presented complaints for counselors and therapists today. Sidney Jourard describes this phenomenon well.

> A choice that confronts everyone at every moment is this: Shall we permit our fellows to know us as we are, or shall we remain enigmas, wishing to be seen as persons we are not? This choice has always been available, but throughout history we have chosen to conceal our authentic being behind masks . . . We camouflage our true being before others to protect ourselves against criticism or rejection. This protection comes at a steep price. When we are not truly known by the other people in our lives, we are misunderstood. When we are misunderstood, especially by family and friends, we join the 'lonely crowd.' Worse, when we succeed in hiding our being from others, we tend to lose touch with our real selves.

When we hide our true selves under the façade of the false self, we cannot experience true intimacy. People don't respond to our authentic self, but simply to the self we project and intend them to see. And while we may gain recognition and praise for our false-self performances and achievements, we know somewhere deep down inside that others don't really know us. In truth, we long ago lost sight of who we really are. All we know consciously is that we don't feel satisfied or fulfilled, nor do we feel truly understood.

A pervasive and persistently held human belief is this: "If you really knew me, you wouldn't like me." Allowing ourselves to believe such a thing is one reason why so much applause falls on deaf ears, and why many of us find it almost impossible to accept praise. The "highs" we experience at moments of recognition are short-lived and deeply doubted. Our fears continue to nag us: "I'm not really worth anything," or, "They were just saying that to be nice," or, "It was the polite thing to do."

Stress and Illness

Conceivably, any part of the body can become a target for stress-related illness. Our everyday language is full of references to the relationship between stress and physical symptoms. Consider these references to the gastrointestinal system: "You may be biting off more than you can chew." "I can't swallow what's going on at the office." "I can't stomach the new boss." "He doesn't have the guts to stand up for himself." Other parts of the body figure in similar expressions. Within medical circles there is a widely held suspicion that these are more than just metaphorical phrases. Most health professionals now believe that stress is a major precursor for medical complaints and serious illnesses. Certainly environmental conditions and genetic predispositions play their part, but what actually triggers the illness?

Researchers have demonstrated a relationship between stress and cardiovascular disorders. We've all heard about people who "don't have their heart in their work" or "don't have the heart to tell the boss what they really think" about the latest missed promotion or the decision to freeze salaries for another year. Hypertension — high blood pressure — is often associated with stress. This symptom can be aggravated when people are under "too much pressure."

The musculoskeletal system is another prime target for stress-related symptoms. "You'll be sticking your neck out if you tell them what you really think." "My boss is a pain in the neck." "He doesn't have the backbone to stand up for what he knows is right." Or, "If she does that, she won't have a leg to stand on." Other common phrases are: "You look like you're carrying the weight of the world on your shoulders," or "Don't stoop to their level." Some physicians have suggested that nearly ninety percent of lower back pain is stress-related. Many people hold tension in their muscles. Some grind their teeth from stress, or develop jaw pain from clenching their teeth — it's a distinct possibility when you're holding back something you really want to say!

Even the largest organ, the skin, can manifest symptoms of stress. Certain types of hives or rashes may be related to something a person is "itching" to say or do, but won't. Perhaps someone has "rubbed them the wrong way."

Are all of these phrases merely figures of speech? Are there no connections between what we say and how we feel? There is too much evidence to support the reality that the body's systems are affected negatively and often painfully by emotions that are not directly acknowledged or expressed.

Rather than physical symptoms, some of us experience vague feelings of emptiness, loneliness, and restlessness, accompanied by confused longings and strivings. These can evolve into compulsions, obsessions, and phobias, often with physical manifestations. Emptiness can be experienced as hunger, thirst, a craving for material things and for excitement. Boredom is often experienced as a lusting and overwhelming drive for risk-taking and adventure. Compulsions can range from excess eating, drinking, drugging, working, talking, sex, smoking, and gambling, to a whole host of other self-defeating behaviors. The one common element for all compulsive behaviors is the person's experience of being out of control. The very addictive habit that's being used to gain some sense of security, certainty, stability and control is itself insecure, uncertain, unstable, and out of control.

Giving Up Control

The majority of mutual-help recovery support groups agree that in order to get better, the addict must admit he is powerless over the addictive substance or behavior. The need to be always in control is itself an addiction — an addiction cleverly devised by the false self to avoid the fear of not being in control. For, in our world, being in control is one way to gain self-esteem, and being out of control is seen as a sign of weakness and inadequacy. And yet, the suffering person is amazed to discover that, once he or she becomes able to admit to being out of control, a pathway opens that leads to an entirely new, and more fulfilling, way of life. Authenticity sets in!

There is one addiction, however, that has found favor in Western civilization. It is the addiction to work. Workaholics are rewarded for their addictive pattern, because it benefits the corporation and generates revenue for the individual and his or her family. In a greed-driven materialistic society, an addiction to work appears to be the perfect adaptation for survival. Nevertheless, scratching beneath the surface often reveals the damages wrought by this particular addiction. Some are similar to those already mentioned. Others can include an aching spouse and scarred children, who may be hidden from the public eye. Many top executives and upper-level managers who share this addiction would laugh at the mere implication that their work is an addiction that is costing them a great deal. They would assume that anyone making such an accusation is simply jealous, uninformed, or suffering from some emotional problem far more severe than a compulsive disorder. With this addiction, as with all others, denial is one of its chief characteristics.

Surface Solutions

If we would take the time to examine and understand the high cost of these physical and emotional symptoms of stress, both in dollars and in human lives, progress could be made toward changing the underlying pathology. Instead, we focus merely on symptom relief. Western civilization plays pharmacological roulette in its efforts to relieve stress-induced insomnia, back pain, headaches, fatigue, restlessness, certain forms of depression, anxiety, addictions, and a plethora of nameless vague symptoms in pursuit of a chemical cure. We accept most of these symptoms as natural by-products of living near the end of the twentieth century, in the midst of the Information Age. We are led to believe that high stress levels are an inevitable outcome of living in a high-tech, rapidly changing world.

Buying into this myth does not serve us well. Certainly stress is generated in the endless effort to keep up with all the latest information and the newest fads, but why do we feel driven to keep up? We're playing roles! We're trying to live up to ideal images and demands! Remember, the eagle was made for flight in the same way humans are made for transforming creativity. The eagle accepted the image and role of the chicken, just as we accept the imprinting of the vicious circle. The eagle beats its wings on the chicken coop in an effort to free itself. We manifest stress because the creative self cannot be contained by our culture's constructed-self games. Our yearning to know our own worth is a heartfelt hunger to experience the release and freedom of transforming creativity.

In the midst of all our game playing, we lose sight of who we really are and what is really important to us. We forget what matters most, so we try to do everything and be all things to all people. And of course we fail — widening and deepening our own vicious circle, entrapping ourselves in a cage of our own making.

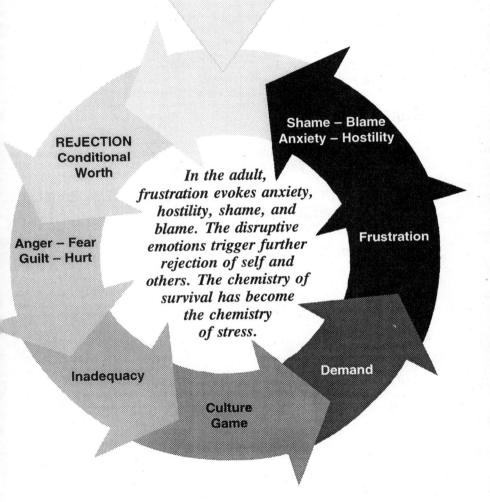

WORTH

REJECTION
Conditional
Worth

Shame – Blame
Anxiety – Hostility

In the adult, frustration evokes anxiety, hostility, shame, and blame. The disruptive emotions trigger further rejection of self and others. The chemistry of survival has become the chemistry of stress.

Anger – Fear
Guilt – Hurt

Frustration

Inadequacy

Demand

Culture
Game

INSIGHT QUESTIONS

Personal Growth:

• How much stress do you have in your life, and what are the sources?

• What do you do for stress relief? Make a list of activities that help you reduce stress.

Relationships:

• Which of your relationships are stressful? Which ones are relaxing and relatively stress-free? Make two lists.

• What can you learn from your stress-free relationships that can help improve the stressful relationships?

Organizations:

• How do your organization's policies and procedures promote stress?

• What stress-reducing efforts are underway at your workplace?

• What recommendations can you make to reduce workplace stress?

10

Mass Producing Mediocrity

"When the eagles are silent, the parrots begin to jabber."
— Winston Churchill

His curly blond hair, blue eyes, and freckles would capture anyone's eye. His style was reminiscent of Huckleberry Finn — right down to the mischievous twinkle in his eye when he grinned. When he wasn't outside catching bugs and small reptiles to bring in the house and delight his mother, he could usually be found in his room thinking about dinosaurs — dinosaurs of every type and from every era. Although only five years of age, Bradley was a dinosaur expert! He had already warehoused in his little mind more information about dinosaurs than most well-educated adults had ever read.

Bradley adored dinosaurs. He knew the correct names (including the pronunciation) of numerous types, their preferred diet, the era in which they flourished, and their approximate size in relation to houses, buildings, and trees of today. He had plastic dinosaur statues that accompanied him in the bathtub at night and occasionally followed him to bed. He wore dinosaur pajamas, slept in dinosaur sheets, read dinosaur books, and ate dinosaur-shaped pasta for lunch on good days. This was not a passing fad for Bradley. His last three birthday parties were orchestrated around a dinosaur theme.

On Bradley's first day of kindergarten, he stood across the street from the school with his father waiting for the crossing guard to signal it was safe to proceed. But Bradley wasn't attending to the guard. Instead, his eyes were firmly fixed on the large brick structure that towered in front of him. It's so *big, he thought with a gulp. "I'd say my new school is about as tall as a full-grown Tyrannosaurus Rex. What do you think, Dad?" His father agreed, and Bradley squeezed his hand as they crossed the street and entered this new world.*

Bradley's teacher was very nice and his classroom was very loud. Twenty-eight other children started kindergarten with Bradley that day. As Bradley stood in the doorway, lunch box in hand, surveying the room, he heard his teacher explain to his father that "this class would be a challenge." Bradley's school was located near a university, and many of his class-mates were the children of graduate students from around the world. English was a second language for at least half of the class. Few, if any of the children had attended formal day care or preschool. Washington Elementary's full-day kindergarten program was a stretch for most of the youngsters and a for-midable task for the teacher — especially without the aid of an assistant. Most days, crowd and noise control was the major goal. Bradley appreciated the retreat home at the end of each day, where he enjoyed a snack and the silent company of dinosaurs.

One day, Bradley's teacher announced that it was time to color a picture and began distributing a piece of paper to each child. Bradley retrieved his crayon box from the desk and waited patiently for his paper. As the teacher passed by, she placed in front of Bradley the most wonderful picture imagin-able — a dinosaur! More specifically, a dinosaur chewing leaves. Most likely a Brachiosaurus, Bradley thought, although the tail was not quite drawn in correct proportion to the body. Despite the minor graphic flaws, Bradley began to color his picture with great enthusiasm.

The teacher was walking around the room to monitor the students' work and maintain order in the classroom. At the end of a very hectic day, patience and energy were in short supply. She paused behind Bradley and abruptly inquired, "Bradley, what on earth are you doing?"

"I'm coloring my dinosaur," he replied.

"But why are you coloring it like that?" she snapped. "Everyone knows dinosaurs don't look like that!"

Bradley looked down at his purple dinosaur with pink spots.

He was pleased with his picture and perplexed by his teacher's declaration. "Well, actually," he stammered, "nobody really knows what dinosaurs looked like on the outside. They might have been green or brown because of where they lived and what they ate. But all anyone has ever seen is a skeleton. No one really knows the color of their skin."

Silence fell, accompanying a harsh and disapproving look on his teacher's face. Bradley's purple and pink dinosaur was swept up, crumpled, discarded and replaced with a fresh, black and white copy. "Begin again!" his teacher ordered, "And this time, do it right."

As Bradley sat and stared at his new paper, his feet dangling and his untied shoelace dragging back and forth across the floor, a small tear trickled across his freckles, fell, and left a wet spot on his page. "Dinosaurs are brown or green," he whispered to himself, "I've got to remember that."

A colleague of ours, Ms. Donna Palmer, who has worked in education and studied educational systems for many years, takes a unique approach. In addition to staying abreast of what educators say about their own field, Donna listens to the kids. She asks children of all ages what they want from their education — what they need from their schools. Their answers are amazing. Children are relatively clear about what they want and need, and their answers are not all "fun and games." They've raised issues ranging from advanced mathematics and science to social and emotional support and nurturing. The sad side to Donna's research and experience is the conclusion she's drawn about education. In the vast majority of our schools, she believes, we successfully eliminate or severely inhibit two innate characteristics of our children — curiosity and creativity. Apparently, we accomplish this task within the first few years of formal education.

Lifelong learning requires curiosity and the ability to be inspired to discover and explore. Losing or inhibiting this trait in children makes the entire educational process a laborious endeavor, ending when the child drops out or meets the minimum requirements for graduation. And yet we find that corporations everywhere are thirsty for "creative types." Creativity is not a chromosomal characteristic reserved for a select few. Children are born creative. They are born to experience the creative expansion of what they can know, appreciate, imagine, and control.

To be creative has at least two meanings. One meaning is the one we have been emphasizing throughout this book — an innate capacity to participate in life-enhancing transformation. This participation leads to the second type — the ability to invent what to do when you don't know. Ten minutes observing a toddler at play will demonstrate that creativity is alive and well in the very young. It is often their persistent creativity that drives adults crazy! Parenting, day care, and formal education methods that require compliance with a strict set of rules and behaviors (demands and expectations) push creative tendencies into dormancy, until, as adults, our efforts have been carefully controlled and molded until they are no longer creative. Our efforts become, not something new and different, but merely a reflection of the norm. We have the ability to be creative; we've just forgotten how. We need to be reminded.

Consider the boy in the story and recall your own educational experiences. Perhaps your teachers were like his — controlling and conforming. Obviously, it is easier for the teacher to control all those bundles of energy if she can squelch the ravenous curiosity that causes children to get into things they shouldn't and inhibit the creativity that leads to a wildly unpredictable day. Of course, it was not the teacher's intent to squelch curiosity and obstruct creativity; she had good intentions to keep things calm and get through the day's work without too many crises. Her methods reflected her own demands and expectations, however, and the need to have those met: "We will get through the lesson plan as it is prepared (whether or not an alternative, exciting opportunity for learning becomes apparent!)."

Remember how you were graded in school? When your teacher returned a homework assignment, quiz, or test, what did the marks on the page highlight? For most people, the marks drew attention to what they did wrong — not what they did right. Red checkmarks or X's were carefully placed to draw attention to your inadequacies. While this was probably not your teacher's intent, in the midst of the culture game as you struggled to gain worth (the worth you never really lost, but believed you did), the marks and many other features of formal education only served to let you know how much more you had to prove. Even on a high-scoring paper, the marks were the first place you looked.

Although traditional educators may have very good intentions, the system serves to reinforce the vicious circle, particularly for any student who struggles with school. If you're not good at learning from books or simply can't transfer your knowledge on a paper-and-pencil test, you're in trouble. Today we label many of these children "learning disabled," yet they may merely have unique learning styles or differences from the majority. In any case, we label them with a disability. As the number of children identified as learning disabled grows, we may soon discover that what we thought was the "normal" or majority learning style did not represent a majority after all.

Maybe you were lucky and had teachers more tolerant or even encouraging of creative diversity. Some marvelous efforts are occurring around the country where teachers and administrators carefully address the needs of the child first and work hard to keep curiosity and creativity alive. To those of us educated in a traditional school system, these schools and classrooms can look like a perfect example of chaos. Yet if you ask the children, they very often love their school, can't wait to go, hate holidays away from school, and are ravenous learners.

Of course, educators are not solely responsible for children's distorted struggle for worth. Parents, childcare providers, grandparents, and other relatives all enforce their own demands and expectations on the child, attempting to inform the child of what is acceptable and what is not. For behaviors deemed unacceptable, the child learns first very basic forms and later more advanced forms of the culture game to keep those inadequacies hidden from view. In the process, the original, creative self becomes increasingly difficult to discern.

During the socialization process we learn that some things are "right" and others are "wrong." In fact, the hallmark of the illusory constructed self is an "either/or" form of consciousness. We tend to view the world and everything and everyone in it from a black/white, good/bad, yes/no, win/lose, right/wrong, and fact/fiction mindset. The result, for many situations and issues, is a debate orientation. You've seen this scenario. Two people begin a conversation in discussion mode; that is, each one expresses an opinion, while neither one really changes the other's view. Differences of opinion quickly turn adversarial, until the pair find themselves embroiled in a debate. The rules of the game change, especially if anyone else is watching. Now, each person strives to express the virtues of his own position and the foibles of the other view. The assumptions: Someone is right. Someone is wrong. Someone will win. Someone will lose. Being right becomes more important than discovering truth. Winning at any cost overrides fair play or justice. The "either/or" mindset is at the heart of many divisions, arguments, and much of the violence that plagues persons, families, institutions, and nations.

The "either/or" polarization process and argumentative mindset work against cooperation and team efforts by hindering integration of ideas and creativity. They limit optimal use of personal, team, and organizational resources. The "either/or" mindset is expensive and dangerous. Not only does it waste time, money, and energy; it often confuses communication. We already know that people tend to interact so that what is unacceptable about themselves and others doesn't show. When this culture game is coupled with the "either/or" mindset, honesty is replaced by deceptive, manipulative, and trivial forms of communication. Integrity gives way to hypocrisy. Openness turns to rigidity and dogmatism. Mutual respect crumbles in the face of authoritarian power games. Creativity and spontaneity are whittled down to conformity and compliance. All these effects are the results of the need to hide and protect the creative self, coupled with the notion that one way is right and the other is wrong. At the cost of authentic interacting, inauthentic communication prevails. It's an extremely high price to pay to sustain conventionality and the status quo.

Old and New Paradigms

At the very heart of the "either/or" mindset are the most deeply held beliefs and assumptions of the so-called civilized world. For centuries the world has labored with a prevailing paradigm: *divide, conquer, compete, and consume.* This paradigm has been so successful and deeply rooted that it permeates most of the world's cultures, both East and West. It has guided the primary strategies of the world's armies, politicians, and educators. As a species, we've divided and conquered everything from fields of knowledge to fields of corn to national boundaries, which are constantly being revised with each new conquest. We've divided the races, the sexes, the advantaged and disadvantaged, and every conceivable ethnic group.

In the workplace we've divided work into specialties and sub-specialties, stove-piped functions, layered management, and built hierarchical chains of command. We've demonstrated a desire to conquer in creating win/lose situations. We've talked of developing "a competitive edge" and increasingly consumed natural, human, and material resources as we divide the market into conquerable slices and compete for a bigger piece of the pie. The "divide and conquer" theme joined to the "either/or" mindset means conquer or be conquered, compete or be consumed. This holds whether we're talking about warring nations, organizing corporations, or playing cards.

The "either/or" mindset assumes an adversarial relationship between business competitors, labor and management, husbands and wives, parents and children, students competing for grades, teachers and principals — the list goes on forever. The "either/or" mindset is at the root of racism, sexism, elitism, nationalism, and a great many other "isms." Once the competition begins, the individual, group, or nation's worth is on the line. Only the fittest have worth, or so it seems. When the illusion takes root that worth must be earned or gained from what we do, how much we accumulate, or whom we know, there is no end to striving for more, better, or quicker. The irony is that while we think there will never be enough, our real worth has been there all along.

The "either/or" mindset is pervasive and endemic. Nevertheless, the mindset itself is a symptom — a symptom of an entire society of individuals struggling to gain a sense of worth out of a sense of self-esteem. It takes many forms — corporate pride, patriotism, racial and ethnic superiority, to name a few. Even when we manage an apparent success with the heightened attendant self-esteem, we know that self-esteem is temporary and conditional, so we must win again and again and again to sustain that self-esteem. Losing makes us try even harder the next time, generating stress and driving us further into a vicious circle to evade the consequences of rejection.

The Costs Are Too High

If we wanted to tally up the financial impact of the "either/or" mindset and stress-related problems, we would have to consider illness, absenteeism, loss of productivity due to debate and confused communication, reduced creativity, and increased violence (both domestic and societal), to name a few. We would need to consider the aggregate impact of these symptoms on the health-care system, the criminal justice system, and business. A conservative estimate may be in the hundreds of billions of dollars. The constructed self's "either/or" consciousness carries a high price for all its claims to success. To measure success without understanding its real cost is not only deceptive, it's dangerous. Instead, we must become able to see that **the vicious circle and the resulting "either/or" mindset sacrifice human transformation towards excellence, in exchange for mass-producing mediocrity.**

Only in recent decades have many begun to understand the interconnectedness of this planet's web of life. Our new understanding of quantum physics and the theories of relativity, chaos theory, and complexity paints a picture of the universe that is vastly different from the Newtonian world we once took for granted. Today's scientific breakthroughs indicate that connectedness, interrelatedness, and interdependency are the rule. A "both/and" mindset is not only possible, it is a more comprehensive reflection of the reality of our universe than the limited "either/or" ever was, a reality that excessive reliance on the "either/or" mindset ignores.

This interconnectedness indicates a very important lesson for us all. While we may have believed we were alone in our struggle for worth, we can now know that we share this vital struggle with every other human being on the planet. Certainly, people experience the struggle to varying degrees, yet it is an experience known to us all. Because this experience is familiar to everyone, escaping the vicious circle by sharing the original self with another original self may not be as threatening as we once thought. There is an alternative to life in the vicious circle. There always has been.

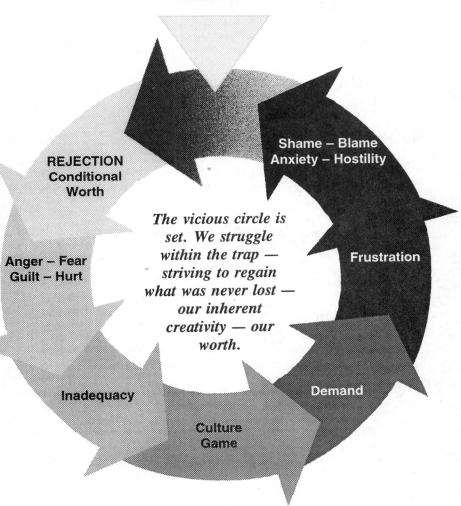

INSIGHT QUESTIONS

Personal Growth:

- How do you divide things, situations, and people into "either/or" categories?

- How willing are you to change your viewpoint once it is established?

Relationships:

- Consider the last time that you had a disagreement with a friend, colleague, or family member. How did you promote an "either/or," a "win/lose"?

- In what ways were you both correct or defending some portion of the truth?

- How could you have achieved a "both/and"?

Organizations:

- How do communication, problem solving, and decision making reflect the "either/or" mindset in your organization?

- What efforts can you make to reverse this trend and enable "both/and" solutions?

Part 2

Cooped Up:

Living the Conspiracy

11

" . . . And They Lived Happily Ever After"

*"I'd like to live in the fast lane,
but I'm married to a speed bump."*

— Barbara Johnson

The couple entered the office and sat at opposite ends of the couch, making more eye contact with the floor and me than they did with one another. I had spoken with each of them separately before. Now they were meeting with me together for the first time.

Their problem was not new — a couple trying to save their marriage and provide a home for their children. Steve had been married once before. His first wife developed cancer and died. He grieved her for quite a while before seeing others. He was a successful businessman when he met Carol, at least successful in the eyes of the world. He had an executive-level position, a great salary, and good benefits, and he was hopelessly unhappy.

Early in their relationship, being with Carol made him believe that he could do anything. She gave him the confidence to throw away the trappings of the corporate life and do what he really wanted. So he did. He quit the job and began his own business. Unfortunately, the business never really got off the ground. So he switched to another. So far the work was very piecemeal. At fifty years of age, the time in his life when he was supposed to have a stable career and a predictable income, he had neither. The "breadwinner" and the "man takes care of the family" scenarios replayed themselves incessantly in his mind — paralyzing him to correct his fate.

" . . . And They Lived Happily Ever After"

Carol had been married before, too. Her marriage ended in divorce, at which time she vowed that she would never make the same mistake again. Now she wasn't so sure. She was tormented by self-accusations: "How could I have been so stupid as to pick the wrong one again? Other people are able to choose the right mate. What's wrong with me? Perhaps that's it. There's nothing wrong with him. It's all me." Whenever this happened, she quickly repressed the thoughts, solidified her conviction that he was the problem, and allowed her anger to grow. Did she love him any more? She wasn't sure. She worked endlessly to maintain a high standard of living for the family. She was good at her job, one of the best. And she hated every moment of it.

Steve and Carol had an agreement. Once they had children, she would gradually decrease her workload and eventually stay at home to be a full-time mom. It wasn't happening. The years were ticking by. The children were growing. She would miss it all. He hadn't kept his end of the deal!

Carol sat cross-legged, trying to reduce her stress by making light conversation and using her quick and sometimes sarcastic humor to bounce the conversation towards any topic that came to mind — anything to avoid the painful topic we all knew must be discussed. Steve sat with crossed arms and handled his stress by conveying an effortful impression of being in control and sincerely getting to the root of their problems. His brow was furrowed, and he looked intensely at me and the carpet, while his arms protected himself from harm.

Each was convinced that the key to changing their relationship required the other to become more tolerant, open, and understanding. Both felt misunderstood and unappreciated. Both considered the other unfair and excessively demanding. Each of them believed they were doing their part to make the marriage work. And they declared they would work harder — if the other partner would take some initiative.

Neither Steve nor Carol could open up to really enter the other's space and really listen to the other's position. Each felt that to do so would be a matter of giving in and losing face. Each one blamed the other for their difficulties. Each saw the other as the cause of what they were feeling. He saw her as too emotional and not rational enough. She saw him as aloof and indifferent — unable to feel.

It took little provocation for Carol to elicit a defensive response from her husband. The topic was the perennial favorite — family finances. She felt justified spending money, as she was the major contributor to the budget. He was more controlling of the expenditures and wanted to save and invest more of both incomes. Steve perceived Carol as extravagant in her purchases, and Carol experienced Steve as a controlling tightwad. Both felt attacked by the other, and both accused the other of insensitivity. It was the classic case of control and countercontrol.

This story is a variation of a story enacted millions of times between married couples whose relationships suffer. The circumstances and the histories of the players may differ, but the issue remains the same. Both partners long to experience the free flight of the eagle within, but feel trapped in another person's demands. Each wants to experience the growth of creative transformation, but converts the drive to fly into the desire to acquire, accumulate, and consume to gain self-esteem. Trapped within the vicious circle of conditional worth and frustrated efforts to earn worth, each person works harder and harder to get the other to conform to his or her demands and expectations. These negative cycles of rejection, inadequacy, games, demands, and stress feed off one another, creating the momentum that can eventually destroy the relationship. It isn't hopeless, however. In fact, there is a great deal of hope. The next step involves risk.

Steve already feels inadequate about his inability to provide for his wife and children. He was probably raised in a traditional home, where the father worked and the mother raised the children. All the modeling and messages of his childhood indicated that a good father was one who provided for his family. The ideal husband and father images were firmly rooted in his mind, with corresponding demands and expectations, which he promptly applied to himself. There is just one problem: he isn't living up to them. His demands on himself are frustrated, and the resulting stress is unbearable. He feels hostile most of the time and catches himself lashing out at Carol, the children, and others — providing 50,000 units of hostility in a situation that calls for 1,000 of anger at most. The guilt and shame that follow demonstrate that, indeed, he does have feelings — terribly uncomfortable ones.

So Steve vows to work harder. Small successes are not enough. He has to attain the ideal to be happy, and as he meets others and observes their life styles, his ideal image grows ever more extravagant. The higher he raises the bar, the more anxiety and hostility he feels about his inability to jump over it. Steve is caught in his own vicious circle.

Of course, Carol is caught in her own vicious circle as well. She, too, was probably raised in a traditional household with the mother at home, sewing, baking, and preparing delicious meals for the family each night. The children were likely bathed and in bed on time every school night without fail (at least, according to Carol's perceptions). Carol's image of the ideal wife and mother does not include rushing home from work by 6:00 and feeling too exhausted to cook, Saturday morning meetings at the office, and occasional overnight business trips. Her image does not include fast-food restaurants, day-care centers, and dependence on others to take over in her absence. Intellectually she knows that the family doesn't need such a high standard of living. She could work less, perhaps even find a less stressful job, and they could still make ends meet. Doing so might necessitate selling the house and moving to more modest quarters, but it is possible. Nevertheless, Carol also has ideal images for life style, private schooling, and the desirable social circles. So she concludes that she really can't leave her job after all. Carol is a victim of her own vicious circle. She's trapped, believing she has no options but to wait for her husband to save the day.

While she waits, she prods. The simplest questions like, "How's the new business coming, Steve?" trigger his vicious circle. He believes he's a failure but works hard to keep it hidden. Questions like this cut right through and expose him, triggering his sense of inadequacy. His response is anxiety and evasion. He gives a lame answer and shifts the spotlight onto Carol: "Why don't you take care of feeding the kids? They need to see their mother now and then." Bullseye! Carol's vicious circle has been triggered. Implying she is a "bad" mother is a sure hook.

The vicious circle is alive and well. Both individuals are trapped, and they continue to trigger one another's pain by exposing one another's inadequacies. Both want to maintain their respective places in the pecking order that will provide self-esteem. Neither can really listen to the other. Both are too caged in their own world of ideal images, demands, and expectations to let down their guard and really hear what the other needs to say.

What would happen if one of them decided to open up and risk rejection? It's a big risk, but it can be done. Suppose that Steve decides to let go of his pride, his ego, and need to perform, and instead puts himself in his wife's shoes. As she talks, he listens. He works hard to avoid blaming himself for her sorrow and, instead, just listens. When she's through, he repeats what he's heard. He tells her why her feelings are important, even though they are painful to hear. He wants to help alleviate her pain, but has no immediate answers. Or does he?

Carol's face appears more relieved — already softened by his response. She's amazed that she's been heard and feels satisfaction for the first time in years at getting her feelings out. So she reciprocates. As she listens to Steve, she, too, works hard not to be hooked by her own inadequacies in relationship to him and instead just listens. She repeats to him what she has heard and is coming to understand, and she expresses appreciation for what he is trying to accomplish.

Neither one has all the answers, but they've taken the first major step. By opening up, sharing their original selves at the risk of rejection, by accepting the other without rejection, they have begun the healing process. Obviously, a few moments of listening are insufficient to undo a spiral of negativity that has gone on for years. A great deal of listening and appreciating is required. Yet the first steps have been taken, and hope is renewed. Steve and Carol have glimpsed the possibility of life beyond the cage. It *is* possible to fly more than a few feet off the ground. There *is* something beyond "chickenhood." Being really heard and accepted for oneself feels good, and it's not the same as self-esteem — it's much more.

INSIGHT QUESTIONS

Personal Growth:

- Think about one or more persons who you feel really listen to you. What is unique in the way they listen? What do they do, what do they say, that makes you feel heard? Make a list of the things they do.

- Commit to practice those same skills in your relationships for one week and see if it makes a difference in strengthening the relationships.

Relationships:

- It is often said that you are lucky if you've had one special friend with whom you could share anything and still be accepted. Have you had such a friend? Would you know how to seek other friends who are just as accepting? If so, how?

- Some people think it takes a long time to develop authentic relationships. Is it really time that matters, or is it the honesty of what you share and how you genuinely listen to one another? What do you think?

Organizations:

- The number-one complaint about managers during the last two decades has been, "They just don't listen." How are good listening skills identified, practiced, and encouraged in your organization?

- What can you do to make a difference in this trend?

12

"Most Likely To Succeed"

"Ours is a world where people don't know what they want and are willing to go through hell to get it."

— Don Marquis

Peter is an experienced consultant for a reputable New Jersey firm. He joined the firm eight years ago after earning both an MBA and a PhD in organization development. Having all the right credentials, Peter had been heavily recruited by a number of firms, but he chose this firm for two reasons: the possibility of becoming a principal (or partner) within nine or ten years, and his desire to remain near his family, who lived in the area.

His peers considered Peter a bit of a hot shot. He didn't have an attitude; he was just good! He worked on the big deals and was instrumental in the success of many projects. The principals of the firm viewed him as a "keeper," and barring any unforeseen catastrophe, he would become a principal himself at the beginning of his ninth year.

Everything seemed to be going as planned. Compared to his high-school buddies and many of his college friends, Peter was doing quite well. Yet, during the last few years, Peter experienced varying waves of emotions about his career. Sometimes he was highly motivated, productive, focused, and fulfilled with a job well done. Other times he couldn't seem to accomplish anything. Concentration was beyond his grasp. He found it much easier to daydream about his woodworking projects at home in the garage than to think about the work on the desk in front of him and the phone calls to be made.

"Most Likely to Succeed"

Peter had always been a highly motivated, disciplined, achievement-oriented person. These periods of mild depression and lack of inspiration alarmed him. He found himself in a state of panic and attempted to work twice as hard to regain his momentum. Yet he discovered that trying to work harder when he really didn't want to work at all was a losing battle.

He knew that, to be invited to be a principal in the firm, one needed to cultivate new clients, not merely work with existing ones. Peter had begun this process with moderate success. He had no big clients yet, but he had a few small ones he could call his own. One such client was his older brother, who owned a die-casting company in the area. They made parts for automobiles, farm equipment, cameras, guns — you name it. It was a small but thriving business. Whenever Peter's brother had personnel, management, scheduling, production, transportation, or any other problem, he called in Peter to solve it. This occurred with some frequency. Peter did his best on these occasions. Most of the time he was very effective in resolving the problem, but the solution was never fast enough or inexpensive enough to suit his brother. Peter felt unappreciated and often angry about this. He wanted to work miracles for his brother. He wanted to impress him with his ability to turn a business around. But opportunities for miracles seemed rare in this die-casting business.

Peter's anxiety and depression climbed. His last cycle of lost productivity and fleeting motivation lasted three months — longer than any previous bout. In fact, each time he fell into a slump, it lasted longer than the one before. During the past six months, Peter had struggled through the flu, a nasty cold, and a lingering case of bronchitis — more illness than he had experienced in the previous three years. Was this a part of getting older, or was it something else? As he sat at his desk and pondered this question, he felt a familiar gnawing feeling in his stomach.

Have you ever gotten something that you wanted for a long time — couldn't wait to get it, dreamt about it all the time — only to discover that, once you had it, it wasn't so great or so impressive after all? Did you find that it didn't make you as happy as you had anticipated? This happens to many of us. Whether it's a small material item, a certain car, a dream house, or the ideal career, somehow it fails to provide the fulfillment and pleasure we were once so certain that it would.

Peter's story is not new or even original. Perhaps you hear some of your friends in this story. Perhaps you hear yourself.

Peter, like everyone else, had long ago become convinced that his worth was conditional. He learned that he should keep his inadequacies to himself and away from public view. Peter had learned to play the culture game. He did all the right things, earned all the right degrees, and learned to "dress sharp" and "talk smart," becoming his ideal image of a successful young executive. He had visions of really doing it up right. He would stand out above the rest. He would be granted rewards earlier than his colleagues. He would set records at his place of business.

Now, having attained some of these ideals, Peter was finding that his stomach ached much of the time, as if it were twisted in knots. He felt uninspired and unfulfilled. Something was missing.

What Peter was missing was his creative self: the keeper of the hopes and dreams nearest to his heart. He had lost touch with the eagle within. He hadn't heard from or listened to that part of himself in many years. He was too caught up in the game to stop and listen. Now he had a vague sense that something was wrong, but his vicious circle kept him hammering away to achieve his demands and expectations, even with mounting stress and physical problems.

Peter's need is not so much to share his original self with others as it is to become honest with himself. Sure, talking openly with others would help, but Peter needs to open up to himself. What does he really want? So what if he chose the wrong career? He made choices a long time ago that are playing out now. How could he have known? Or, maybe consulting is still his field, if he could just let go of his self-imposed demands to stand out among the rest — to always be on a pedestal. After all, when you're on a pedestal, you have much farther to fall!

But to Peter it wasn't OK to ask these questions and follow their potential answers. Stopping everything, switching gears, changing careers, or, at a minimum, working very differently was not acceptable. It wasn't the way one gets to the top of the pecking order. That would be like admitting to everyone — his friends, his brother, and his peers — that he'd made a mistake, he had made the wrong choice, didn't really "have it all together." This would destroy the image, exposing him as a person with faults. No, it was not an option, simply not an option.

Why wasn't it an option? We once knew a young man working for a large law firm who did just that. In the middle of his seventh year, he said, "Stop everything. This isn't for me. While I enjoy the law and the thinking it requires, practicing law in a large firm is not what I expected." So he left. For one year he worked as a juvenile-court judge, hearing a variety of cases from kids who were caught for theft to kids who simply didn't go to school. During that year he had a bit of time to think. He loved sports and was himself very active. After the year of reflection and preparation, he gained a position as counsel for a professional football team. No, life isn't perfect, but it's better. He enjoys his work and feels more "like himself" than he has in years.

Of course, he was ridiculed when he left. People whispered and some even said out loud that he left because he "couldn't cut it" — that he didn't have what it took to be a successful attorney, or couldn't cope with the stress. Others said confidently, "He'll be back" (implying, once he realizes his mistake). Were they really talking about him, or making a statement about themselves?

Some of those who talked had questioned their own career choice at one time or another. They too had experienced periods of burnout and unhappiness. But they stuck it out because that's what disciplined, determined, successful people do! Successful people don't quit! At least, that's what they believed. The voice of the constructed self rings loud and clear. Some people remain in the wrong job for a lifetime, never understanding that they might be better suited for something else.

Peter still has time. He must begin with a clear examination of his values. What is really important to him — not just what he thought was supposed to be important? Is his current job fulfilling those values? If not, can it be altered to better represent Peter's creative self, or is a new career in store?

These questions are not terribly difficult to answer. Most people are just scared to death even to ask them. For if we ask them, we may discover that we were wrong. Being wrong means being inadequate, and being inadequate means putting our worth on the line. The vicious circle plays itself out so strongly in the lives of many people that they won't even let themselves think about ideas, ask questions, or expose topics that are beyond their current demands and expectations. Yet, like Steve and Carol, taking a risk is all that's required for a new world of opportunity to reveal itself.

INSIGHT QUESTIONS

Personal Growth:

- Estimates suggest that over ninety percent of Americans are unhappy in their current employment. Are you one of those people?

- What performance expectations do you have for yourself that force you to stay in a position that is neither satisfying nor fulfilling?

- Take a few moments to examine these performance demands. Is this the way you want to spend the rest of your life?

Relationships:

- Think of someone close to you over whom you have some influence — a child or a friend, for example. What performance expectations do you have for them? Make a list.

- In what ways might you be encouraging that person to be someone they're not?

- What could you do to help them discover their innate creativity — the eagle within?

Organizations:

- How does your organization reward performance?

- How does your organization acknowledge worth?

13

"The Learning Organization"

*"When fear replaces passion in the creative process,
that means it's the end of the process."*

— Scott Burns

This group had a reputation, and Raymond knew it in advance. All their corporate propaganda painted the picture of a learning organization. "We work hard to encourage diversity," they would say. "We believe that new and different ideas are the key to our success now and in the future." Operating in the chemical industry, they realized that effective teaming, open communication, and creative thinking were among their key success factors. In order to enhance these skills and foster genuine leadership abilities, they assembled their top managers for a series of workshops and seminars stretched out over an eleven-month period.

The learning-organization theme, despite all their brochures and statements to this effect, was not the reputation that preceded them. The course of training involved meeting several days per month, during which some of the best thinkers on leadership, teaming, and organizational change paraded through to teach their concepts and practices.

Raymond, today's speaker, was the fourth in a series. Warnings had come from the previous months' speakers: "This is a highly dysfunctional group! They enjoy eating consultants for lunch!" Evidently, some of the speakers had been verbally assaulted and their material attacked. Most of them muddled through, quietly making their points until they could leave, while some never finished but just left prematurely.

"The Learning Organization"

"What about all that 'learning organization' talk? Oh well, never mind," thought Raymond. After all, he was very experienced. With over twenty-five years in the business, he had worked with a wide range of teams. This group would be fine.

Nineteen people gathered on the first day. While all were in management positions, two men were managers of all the others in the room. You knew that as soon as they walked in. Apparently, it was their intent to make known who they were. They were quite a pair. Their voices were loud and boisterous. They walked amongst the group making verbal jabs and slapping the backs of their subordinates. There would be no question as to who was in charge.

Evidently Raymond needed to learn this lesson, too. When he attempted to call the room to order to begin the day's work, the two senior managers let him know that the session would begin when they decided it was time. Within a few seconds, it was time. Evidently, they just needed to call the shots.

As Raymond began, he studied the faces in the group. The majority of them looked humbled by their bosses' behavior and eager to hear the new information being shared. Others kept their eyes on their papers and rarely made eye contact with anyone in the room. The two senior men sat in the back, arms crossed, tilting their chairs back to rest on the back legs, and wore calculating smirks on their faces.

Then the questions began. At first, the two top men asked normal, expected questions about the material presented. Upon answering them, Raymond realized he'd been set up for an attack. No matter what answer he gave, they clearly intended to take him on. Raymond was experienced with this as well. He answered the questions, defended his ideas against the attacks, and attempted to move on to the rest of the material.

Then the attacks changed, becoming personal in nature. His presentation style, the way he talked, the way he looked, the suit he chose were all fair game for the two bullying managers. For them, it was like a contest. They enjoyed playing off one another, outdoing one another to see who could *make the most piercing statement and throw Raymond off guard. Raymond was clearly annoyed with the tone and the aggressiveness of the two. He was grateful for the lunch break.*

During the meal, Raymond spoke with some of the other team members and learned that this was a common experience, a reflection of everyday life at work. The other participants had hoped this training might begin to change things. Unfortunately, it just seemed to be getting worse. They were miserable realizing that, because of the senior managers, they weren't even hearing much of the valuable information that could be gained from the speakers. Raymond encouraged them to express their concerns to the whole group after lunch. The issue needed to be brought into the open.

At the beginning of the afternoon session, Raymond asked for comments or questions about the material covered so far. One courageous individual decided to raise the issue of the dysfunctionality in the room. "I've been thinking that if we could begin to practice some of the communication skills you suggested this morning, we could solve a lot of our problems, reduce the number of errors made on the job, and probably improve morale."

The two managers seemed startled. One sat straight up in his chair and glared at the speaker. "I think we're doing just fine," he said sternly. "Are you suggesting that we have communication and morale problems?"

Amazed by this young man's courage, Raymond watched him stammer about and state, "Well, yes. I think we have a few areas we could improve upon."

At that point, the manager nearest him moved closer, stood behind the young man, placed a firm hand on his shoulder, and said, "Now, surely you don't think that, do you?"

Silence followed. Diversity successfully squelched, the same manager turned to Raymond and said, "Now, you can go ahead and tell us what you want to say."

As consultants, we're pretty careful not to throw around the word "team" when describing any gathering of people. A team is a collection of people who share a common goal and work cooperatively to achieve it together. There are varying levels of teams, depending on how smoothly, quickly, and creatively they listen and integrate ideas. The individuals in this story do not qualify as a team. They don't even qualify as a group. They are more reflective of a mob — a very controlled, cowed mob, with two dictators at the top.

Yet, this is not a unique mob. If you've ever worked in such an environment, you know how oppressive it feels. You know what to say, what not to say, and how you are expected to respond when asked for input. Some people continue to rebel, often losing their jobs or being transferred. Others sit quietly, hoping for change or looking for a way out.

It's easiest to place the blame for lost productivity, poor quality, obstacles to learning, and ineffective communication on the managers. Their behavior causes them to stand out. Their hostility towards others makes them easy targets. Yet the person behind the hostile mask hurts. For reasons yet unknown, these two men are deeply hurting. There may be any number of circumstantial explanations for their attitudes, but it all boils down to a an overall sense of low self-esteem and worthlessness. In their efforts to regain worth, they have established an intricate web of demands and expectations for their own and others' behavior. They are driven to manipulate every situation in an attempt to recover the control, security, certainty, and stability they've lost. Over time, this backfires. Subordinates and peers dislike and disrespect them. The more isolated they feel, the more aggressively they fight for control.

One of these managers is an alcoholic. His reddish complexion was the first clue. His beverage choices at lunch, the mid-afternoon break, and dinner indicated that the initial perception was accurate. Three stiff drinks at noon were not uncommon for him. Upon returning to the meeting, he was more belligerent and more offensive — his hostility fueled by alcohol. Earlier we discussed the vicious circle as it relates to addictive tendencies. This manager seems unable to control his drinking, so he determines to control everything else — absolutely everything and everyone else.

The two managers play off one another and rationalize their behavior by noting that they're not the only ones acting in this way. Each one perceives the same anger and need to control in the other, so it must not be all bad! And besides, they've remained relatively successful so far. The business continues to do well.

Why should they change? In fact, to their thinking, this may be the ideal culture!

This hypercontrolling, oppressive manner of dealing reinforces their game and triggers the vicious circle in others. Their demands are so strong and forcefully communicated that they are bound to clash with the demands of another person sooner or later. Clearly they dominate, making them a convenient scapegoat for the group. And this is a key insight:

Whenever someone successfully dominates a group, the rest of the members are allowing it to happen. In order to dominate, someone must be willing to be dominated.

The silent members of the group feel trapped. They've seen people lose their jobs for speaking up and challenging one of the managers before. Most of them have families at home who rely on their income. Rather than rock the boat and risk financial security, they play the game and do as they are told, at least until something better comes along.

Helping this group change would be a challenge and focusing on the managers first a likely mistake. The two managers have some very deep hurt that could take years to relieve. The alcoholic manager will likely never change, without treatment for his disease, the filter through which he views the world. The rest of the participants, however, are also contributing to the problem. They are giving the directors exactly what they need to continue the cycle, allowing the destructive culture to permeate all their relationships at work. A healthy dose of authentic interaction between the group's members could go a long way. By talking about the issue with one another, along with the other problems they face as a work group, they can begin to hear, understand, and appreciate the goals and values of their other group members. This is the type of communication that builds community and commitment.

More difficult still would be listening to, understanding, and appreciating the wishes of the managers. Sometimes it takes a saint to look into the face of hostility and try to understand and appreciate. Yet this is what is required. The managers behave as they do because they have lost touch with their own sense of worth. Affirming their worth by taking the time to listen and understand them would be the first step in reducing their hostility. Although it may be difficult to see through the fog of anger, threats, and oppression, these managers must have something valuable to offer. The company would not have survived if they were doing nothing right. The challenge to the team members is to look for the good — affirm the value.

The managers and their subordinates have established a predictable pattern: the managers behave in a controlling, hostile manner, and the others conform, are quiet, or leave. When the team members begin to actively listen to the managers to gain understanding and appreciate the managers for the value they bring to the organization, the predictable pattern is broken. The managers can no longer engage in the oppressive pattern of behavior, because it doesn't work any more. It no longer elicits the same response. In the end, the managers themselves have to try something new. Again, this may be easier said than done, but it is the only solution that brings with it the promise of lasting change.

INSIGHT QUESTIONS

Personal Growth:

• In what situations are you similar to the managers in this story, ensuring that everyone conforms to your standards to gain certainty, stability, security and control?

• In what situations are you similar to the team members, allowing yourself to be controlled by others and refusing to speak up for what you believe?

Relationships:

• In relationships that exhibit some dysfunction, oftentimes people will say in private that there is "an elephant" in the relationship, meaning there is a significant presence or problem. This elephant is usually ignored and not discussed. Do you have some relationships like this?

• It is a form of hypocrisy when we strive to keep the obvious from being addressed. Have you ever avoided these difficult "elephant" subjects in the effort not to hurt someone's feelings or to avoid unpleasant interactions?

• What would it take to increase the authenticity of the relationships and address "the elephant"?

Organizations:

• Many organizations collude and keep dysfunctional people in positions of leadership. This often continues to the detriment of the corporation because the problem is not openly addressed. Is this happening in your organization?

• How are you a part of maintaining the problem — the dysfunction?

• What can you do to break the cycle?

Part 3

Releasing The Eagle Within:

Rediscovering Your Creative Self

14

Unlocking The Cage

"You were born with wings.
Why prefer to crawl through life?"

— Rumi

It was not a happy place. The people in the room, parents and children, were angry, hurt, fearful, and guilty. Everything seemed to be crashing down at once. The kids couldn't believe the trouble they'd gotten into, and the parents were in shock.

The day before, two of the girls had gone for a walk in the park. Upon their return, they went straight to bed and fell asleep. One didn't get up until the next morning; the other crawled out of bed two hours later and went to the kitchen for a drink.

"Why are you so tired?" her mother asked.

"I don't know. I just am," she mumbled.

"Are you feeling OK?"

"No. I mean yes. I'm just tired."

"Come here and look at me. You're not acting right," her mother stated in a concerned voice. She peered into her daughter's eyes. Something wasn't right. Her thirteen-year-old daughter was acting strangely. "Why are your eyes so red?" she asked worriedly.

"I don't know. I guess I've been rubbing them a lot," the girl responded, and turned to walk away.

"Wait a minute. Come back. Something's going on, and I want to know what it is."

The conversation continued. It was a bumpy one. Finally

the truth came out. The girls had bought a small bag of marijuana from a teenage boy they knew, and decided to give it a try that afternoon. The mother was torn. She felt as if she had known it all along, and yet she was in complete shock.

The two girls, their parents, and the teenager who supplied the drug were in the midst of a meeting. This was not a cordial, problem-solving meeting. This was a hostile, hurting group of people, all the participants knowing they had to take some responsibility for the incident and each one wanting to blame it on someone else.

One of the fathers turned to the teenage boy and yelled, "Why did you do this? Why on earth would you sell a drug to twelve- and thirteen-year-old kids?"

Leaning smugly back against the wall, hands in his pocket, a complete poker face, staring straight at the father, he responded, "To make money."

This was not the right answer. The parents' anger sky-rocketed. Verbal threats and attacks flew around the room.

"Hey," the young man yelled above the noise. "I might have sold it, but it was your kid who bought it."

Things weren't getting better; they were getting worse. This little meeting probably wouldn't accomplish much and might see several people regretting what they said. The air was thick. It seemed hard to breathe. The two youngsters looked mostly at their shoes, while their parents hammered away at the boy they saw as responsible for the whole mess. Time seemed to drag. They'd give anything if they could change it all and get out of this pressure cooker.

Then one of the two girls spoke up, "Look," she said slowly and sincerely. "I hear what you're saying. I know that he should have known better than to offer us the pot. But I also know that I should have known better than to buy it. I did the wrong thing, and I'm in trouble for it. It's time to look at the situation for what it is."

The room fell silent. Time seemed almost to stand still with everything frozen in air. At that moment the boy changed. He no longer stood stoic, the detached attacker. His body relaxed, his face softened. He looked at the floor and then

*back at the parents. His blue eyes cradled tears. "I'm sorry,"
he whispered from his gut. "I'm terribly, terribly sorry." The
tears rolled down his face.*

*The thick air became more breathable. The room seemed
less filled with criminals and more like a group of people who
made mistakes and now had a common problem to solve.
The yelling ceased. No more fists shook, and no more fingers
pointed. Those who had risen to their feet sat down.*

*"Well," one father said softly with a sigh, "we just need
to figure out what to do about it now."*

In the marijuana story, something happened in an instant that
changed the tone and direction of the gathering. A girl spoke softly
and from the heart, she shared her original self with others, and,
as her message sank in, it changed the hearts of the others in the
room. The teenage boy found the strength to own his mistake and
express his remorse. The angry father began to see the young
people, not as enemies, but as individuals needing guidance and
support. In a brief moment, something changed that allowed the
people in that room to unravel the vicious circle and begin to
participate in transformation.

Throughout this book, we've told simple stories from daily life.
While they may not be your stories in every detail, they contain
familiar themes. We've told these stories for a precise reason — to
bring to conscious awareness the nature of the vicious circle that
entraps so much human potential and makes chickens of us all.

An old proverb states, "Fish discover water last." Fish are so
continually surrounded by water that they take it for granted — we
assume they don't even perceive it. Likewise, the dynamics of the
vicious circle become imperceptible to us as we shape our lives
more and more around the images and demands of the constructed
self. The grip this destructive dynamic has on our lives becomes
imperceptible, to the point that we believe there is no other possible
reality — no other way to live.

The first purpose of this book is to raise the vicious circle to
awareness, so that we may see it and understand it for what it is.
The second purpose of the book is to point toward the alternative.

Reducing the negative impact of the vicious circle requires us
to pursue both purposes. The **first step** is to focus on the experience

of the vicious circle itself, identifying the cage the moment we're caught in it. We know the vicious circle has been triggered when we experience anxiety, hostility, shame, or blame. Ultimately, these emotions serve as useful warning signals that the vicious circle has been activated. We sometimes label them as "negative" emotions, because they cause "dis-ease" and distress in our lives. Recognizing and naming them, then welcoming their message, is an important first step in escaping this destructive dynamic. Although most people have an inadequate vocabulary of "feeling" words, we can try to be as specific as possible, going deeper than generalities such as happy, sad, good and bad. Rejected, ignored, discounted, hurt, attacked, scared — all these are useful feeling states to be able to identify.

The **second step** is to identify which demand or expectation is being frustrated or blocked. Perhaps someone has not accepted something we believe or value — say, when someone we expect to agree with us disagrees. Such a simple event triggers the possibility that our way of thinking and believing may not be the only way. Worse still, it may suggest that our beliefs are wrong. We may go so far as to conclude that our belief system is inadequate for anyone's needs! Although this is the end result of an irrational expectation, such grandiose demands formulated at a subconscious level are intrinsic to the pursuit of the illusions of stability, certainty, security, and, most of all, control. So, the **third step** is to identify how we experience inadequacy in response to frustrated demands and expectations.

The **fourth step** is critical to interrupting the vicious circle — recognizing how we have put our worth on the line. How have I, or you, seen worth as contingent on being adequate in this situation? At the deepest level of the constructed self, most of us assume we must be adequate in all things with all people all the time, else we have no worth. We make our worth dependent on this ideal of perfection! When we can recognize the ludicrous nature of our dilemma and accept that, in fact, our worth cannot be compromised, we can unlock the vicious circle and address the situation from outside the confines of the cage.

And of course, the **fifth step** is to remember that you and I were born with a full complement of personal worth. It's factory equipment!

5
Worth

4

1. Recognize the Emotion
2. Trace Emotion to Frustrated Demand
3. Connect Demand to Inadequacy
4. Track Inadequacy to Worth
5. Accept Your Worth

1

3

2

Therefore, the pattern for unlocking the cage is:

1. Recognize and identify the disturbing emotion you feel.

2. Identify the frustrated demand or expectation that led to the emotion.

3. Discover how the failed expectation and frustrated demand led to a sense of inadequacy.

4. Notice how you've made your worth dependent on being adequate in this situation.

5. And, finally, accept that your inherent worth is intact and not based on performance, success, or achievement.

In the end, no one ever permanently escapes the vicious circle. Feelings of frustration, inadequacy, and worthlessness are an inevitable part of human experience. Some religious thinkers argue that the vicious circle is equivalent to sin — anything that leaves us in an alienated state. To participate in one's own self-destruction is, for them, the way sin operates in our lives. When we, supposedly made in the image of our Creator, deny our creative selves, according to this doctrine, we engage in sin. To be completely without sin, they suggest, is contradictory to the human experience as we know it. Other religious thinkers speak of a state of "original blessing" — the way we were before the culture indoctrinated us. Still other traditions call these concepts by other names.

Although we will always have moments when we feel inadequate and need affirmation, the vicious circle does not have to dominate our lives leading to frustration, stress, and dis-ease. Life need not be lived within the confines of the culture game and the constructed self. We can choose not to live as chickens. We are designed to be eagles.

As we apply the five steps outlined above, we can focus on reducing the frequency, intensity, and duration of the vicious circle's hold on our lives. Every time the crippling emotions occur, we can recognize and open the cage door by following the steps. Over time, we will discover that our vicious circle is triggered less often, and the intensity of the emotions we feel will also subside.

We are not meant to live life ravaged by extreme hostility and anxiety as the result of perceived loss of worth. Life's greatest illusion need not control us in this way. The more practiced we become in using the steps, the more adept we will become at reducing the amount of time we remain trapped in the vicious circle. The length of time we are consumed by the uncomfortable emotions will diminish, and we can move toward the transforming creativity for which every one of us was designed.

15

Making The Obvious, Obvious

"You must be the change you wish to see in the world."
— Gandhi

"Please Hear What I'm Not Saying"
— Author Unknown

Don't be fooled by me.
Don't be fooled by the mask I wear.
For I wear a mask; I wear a thousand masks; masks that I'm afraid to take off, and none of them are me.
Pretending is an art that is second nature with me, but don't be fooled, for God's sake don't be fooled.
I give the impression that I'm secure, that all is sunny, unruffled, with me, within as well as without; that confidence is my name and coolness is my game; that the waters are calm and that I'm in command, and I need no one.
But don't believe, please don't . . .
Beneath dwells the real me, in confusion, in fear, in loneliness.
But I hide this; I don't want anybody to know it.
I panic at the thought of my weakness and of being exposed.
That's why I frantically create a mask to hide behind, a nonchalant sophisticated façade to help me pretend, to shield from the glance that knows.
But such a glance is precisely my salvation, my only salvation, and I know it.
That is, if that glance is followed by acceptance, if it's followed by love.

The Chicken Conspiracy

It's the only thing that will assure me of what I can't assure myself, that I'm really worth something.

But I don't tell you this. I don't dare. I'm afraid to.

I'm afraid that deep down inside I'm nothing, that I'm just no good, and that you see and reject me.

So I play games, my desperate, pretending games, with a façade of assurance on the outside, and a trembling child within.

And so begins the parade of masks, the glittering but empty parade of masks.

And my life becomes a front.

I idly chatter with you in the suave tones of surface talk.

I tell you everything that's really nothing, nothing of which is everything, of what's crying within me.

So when I'm going through my routine, do not be fooled by what I'm saying.

Please listen carefully and try to hear what I'm not saying; what I'd like to be able to say, what, for survival, I need to say, but I can't say . . .

Each time you are kind and gentle and encouraging, each time you try to understand because you really care, my heart begins to grow wings.

Very small wings.

Very feeble wings, but wings. With your sensitivity and sympathy and your power of understanding, I can make it . . .

So do not pass me by. Please do not pass by. It will not be easy for you.

A long conviction of worthlessness builds strong walls. The nearer you approach me, the blinder I may strike back . . .

Who am I, you may wonder? I am someone you know very well. For I am every man, every woman, every child . . . every human you meet.

It is a rare individual who can not relate to this personal statement. The author, although nameless, is familiar to us all. The human being beneath the façade seeks expression — seeks to be known, heard, and understood — to make a connection with another original soul. Who among us can deny this desire? Gratefully, we have moments in our lives in which we share this experience with another human being — the joy of being loved unconditionally, of being accepted for who we are. Then why do these moments happen so infrequently? Why must these relationships be so rare?

Unlocking the vicious circle, unraveling its deadly hold when we find ourselves in it, is a critical starting point. An even more critical and profound process for escaping the vicious circle is pursuing the transforming creativity available to us all. This transforming creativity must not remain a mystery, becoming instead an active experience in our daily lives. Engaging in transforming creativity occurs through a very simple, innate, and profound process called creative interchange. If the vicious circle is a life-destroying process that produces physical, emotional, psychological, and spiritual dis-ease, creative interchange is the life-giving process that leads to health and wellness — in these very same areas.

We aren't the first to speak of creative interchange. It was identified and described by Henry Nelson Wieman in the early 1900s. Wieman said:

> The ability to learn what others have learned, to appreciate what others appreciate, to feel what others feel, and to add all this to what the individual has acquired from other sources, and finally to form out of it all . . . one's own individuality is what distinguishes the human mind from everything else.
>
> — *Man's Ultimate Commitment*

Wieman's words describe the healthy, transforming process of human growth when it is not confined and obstructed by the vicious circle. To learn what others have learned, to discover value in what they appreciate, and to feel what they feel requires an openness with others not reflective of the controlling, ego-serving vicious circle.

The process of creative interchange in human life is also like the water to the fish. You've engaged in this process many times before, and you will many times again. Like the fish in the water, we're always in it, to varying degrees. We are always in the midst of possibilities for authenticity and creative transformation. The frequency, intensity, and duration with which we experience this life-giving, transforming process depends on our degree of entrapment in the vicious circle. When we significantly reduce the impact of the vicious circle, we gain an increasing experience of our worth through the creative interchange process.

Recognizing Creative Interchange

We know this process best by the results it enables — the self-transformation, large or small, that we experience. It happens whenever we feel a special connection to another human being. It happens when we learn from someone or feel changed positively when interacting with another person. Maybe we met the person face to face, or spoke on the phone, or received a meaningful letter. Creative interchange takes place whenever we interact in an authentic manner, take the time to understand and appreciate one another, and allow ourselves to be influenced and creatively changed by one another.

In questions following earlier chapters, we asked you to reflect on relationships in which you felt really heard by another person, remembering those friendships in which you can say anything you genuinely feel and still be accepted by the other. We also asked you to consider the elements of these relationships in order to repeat them in other aspects of your life. Those meaningful relationships are examples of the creative interchange process at work. Creative interchange is not just about learning something new; it's also about recognizing this healthy, life-giving process and raising it to consciousness, so that you can engage in it more intentionally and consistently. This is an experience of releasing and giving flight to the eagle within. This type of interacting need not be reserved for a select few loved ones and dear friends. This process is available all the time, with everyone we meet. We merely need to become aware of the process and the conditions that foster it, then move ahead to engage in these behaviors in an intentional and consistent way.

Facilitating Creative Interchange

Creative interchange is the dynamic process that brings about transformation in human life. The end result of such transformation is always unknown. We cannot plan in advance the outcome of our own creative change. As Wieman observed, "Creative interchange transforms the human mind as it cannot transform itself." In this way, we cannot control this process. (As we've discovered, the need to control is an outcome of the vicious circle.) In order to engage in creative transformation, we must open ourselves up to the process and engage in those behaviors that foster creative interchange. The behaviors required are neither difficult nor unfamiliar; they are merely different from the habitual patterns established within the trap of the vicious circle. To explore this notion further, let's examine the four major characteristics of creative interchange.

Authentic Interacting

Creative interchange is increased when people interact authentically with one another. Authentic interacting fosters creative interchange, in that we are willing to voice, with integrity, our unique perspectives, thinking, interpretations, beliefs, and values while encouraging others to do the same. Simply put, we share our original creative selves. Whether in an organization, family, school or other setting, we need to share our best ideas, greatest dreams, worst fears, incomplete plans, and all the rest with other human beings. And, at the same time, we need to make room for others to do the same with us.

Making room for others means that we intentionally seek to hear and understand another's viewpoint. It means that we actively inquire into others' ideas — not to debate or contradict, but to understand and learn. This inquiry represents humility regarding my own way of looking at the world, because if I am to learn from someone else, I must give up the effort to have all the answers. Genuine inquiry also indicates that I value both the unique ideas expressed and the unique person sharing them. Authentic interacting is twofold: advocating with integrity for the best we know, and inquiring with humility into the best others know.

Once such interaction begins within a group, diversity quickly surfaces. We discover just how unique each of us is. Lotus®, a business software company, ran an advertisement echoing this thought:

> You are a visionary. You started out knowing not much at all. But you processed everything that anyone ever shared with you. And you shared it back again until you discovered that what you know is different from anyone else in the world.

Sharing openly with one another doesn't create clones; rather, it helps each of us discover that we do indeed have a unique perspective on the world that is worthy of expression.

Appreciative Understanding

As soon as this freed-up diversity surfaces, it becomes critical that we focus on appreciatively understanding the diversity. Both "appreciating" and "understanding" are important words. Many times when we hear something that strikes us as bizarre, our first inclination is to dismiss it immediately and stop listening. We no longer give the subject our time and attention. Appreciative understanding requires, first, that I make sure I have correctly understood what the other is saying. Having done this, I could still say, "Now, that I understand what you're saying I'm *certain* it is the most ridiculous thing I've ever heard!" Not, perhaps, the most productive response. This is where appreciation comes in.

Appreciative understanding means that I seek to discover value in what someone else is expressing. Most of us don't intentionally risk expressing a thought we consider stupid. If I hear an idea and consider it stupid, the problem is as much a function of my own perceptual filters as it is a function of the other person. Appreciating means finding value in another person's point of view. I don't have to agree with what you are saying; I will simply try to understand and appreciate why you see things as you do. Appreciative understanding is not intended to make us all the same; rather, it's about helping every one of us discover our own uniqueness by recognizing appreciatively how unique others are.

Appreciative understanding is about more than just finding what's useful or valuable. It's about fully appreciating all aspects of an idea or point of view — our own and others'. In other words, we may find it equally important to appreciate what is *not* of use or value — the drawbacks. Appreciative understanding means accepting that all ideas — including our own — are made up of both positive aspects and drawbacks. Typically, we are aware of the valuable aspects of our own thinking and easily see the drawbacks or flaws in the thinking of another. When we focus on the strengths of our thinking to the exclusion of the strengths in the thoughts of others, we limit appreciation. At the same time that we overlook the strengths in their perspective, we tend to ignore the weaknesses in our own. In such situations, we see only part of the truth. Appreciative understanding pursues all the positives and drawbacks in every perspective.

By themselves, authentic interacting and appreciative understanding have tremendous power to counteract the culture games characteristic of the vicious circle. Authentic interacting (based on the original, creative self) contradicts the base premise of the culture game. When you are interacting with authenticity, you cannot conceal what might be seen as unacceptable about yourself. Authentic interacting enables the whole self — both its strengths and weaknesses — to become visible. Appreciative understanding of others, particularly those who are very different from us, unravels individual demands and expectations. Appreciative understanding cannot happen while we are trapped in our own demands. When people are openly sharing and appreciating one another, the old self-negating, destructive games can no longer survive.

Creative Integrating

In addition to these two elements, creative interchange allows us to integrate the diversity we bring to one another. Through such integration, we learn and change by taking into our awareness the experiences and values of others. Rather than debating ideas, we invent ways to develop "both/and" opportunities. The desired result is that I can learn something from you and you can learn something from me. One or both of us can experience transformation through this interaction. Antoine de Saint-Exupéry describes the transformation process well with this scene from *The Little Prince,* in which a fox speaks to the prince in the forest.

> And then look: you see the grain-fields down yonder? I do not eat bread. Wheat is of no use to me. The wheat fields have nothing to say to me. And that is sad. But you have hair that is the color of gold. Think how wonderful that will be when you have tamed me! The grain, which is also golden, will bring me back the thought of you. And I shall love to listen to the wind in the wheat.

Through this interchange, the fox is forever changed. Never again will he see the world in quite the same way. For the fox, the wheat fields previously held no value, no interest (much like an idea you don't like or information you disagree with). Yet, through a

CREATIVE INTERCHANGE

Authentic Interacting

Sharing your best knowledge with others and encouraging others to share their best.

Continual Improving

Acting on the best we know and committing to make it better.

Appreciative Understanding

Understanding and finding value in what others understand and value.

Creative Integrating

Building connections within diversity to achieve innovative synergistic results.

process of creative integration, for him the wheat fields have now been transformed and bring new meaning to his life. Never again will he be able to gaze out upon a wheat field without remembering the Little Prince.

During creative integrating, the fruits of true cooperation and synergy become apparent, bringing us to a wonderful realization: **All of us are smarter than any one of us, if we just don't get in each other's way.** Of course, people often do get in each other's way. Only by authentic interacting, appreciatively understanding, and integrating the diversity to create "both/and" or "win/win" outcomes can we maximize the unique talents of people, races, and nations. Through creative interchange, you and I achieve results that are *more than* and *different from* what either of us could achieve working in isolation. We can build on one another's strengths and work together to overcome each other's weaknesses.

Continual Improving

This liberating new approach to ideas is only the beginning. We are also called to put the new learning and innovative ideas to work. This component of creative interchange requires a two-fold commitment. As Wieman pointed out, we must first be committed to "act on the best we now know." All of the innovative solutions and new learning we gain through the creative interchange process must be acted upon to bring about any positive change — personal, organizational, societal, global, or all of these. Only through action can any of us be transformed towards our highest potential good.

Secondly, we must commit to a continual engagement with transforming creativity, refusing to be bound by the constraints of "chickenhood." This transforming creativity, realized through creative interchange, enables the best we currently know to become something even better. Commitment to this process is essential if we are to experience progressive expansion of what we can know, appreciate, imagine, and do. Such a commitment requires us to look discerningly at today's fad or latest invention, in order not to obstruct further learning, growth, and creative transformation. In other words, we must not stop with today's *created good* or best, but rather commit ourselves to *creative good* — the creative process that enables the ongoing transformation of human life.

Learning to Fly

We have a very dear friend who reads ravenously. His wife tells us that upon finishing a particularly meaningful book, he will typically close the cover and say with a sigh, "Wow! This book has changed my life!" leaving his wife to mumble to herself, "Sure. I'll believe it when I see it." This has probably happened to you; it happens to all of us. We come across something new that seems valuable, and we have every intention to make it a new habit. Our challenge lies in translating all our good intentions into a daily way of life.

Stepping out of the vicious circle to engage consistently and consciously in creative interchange won't just happen because of good intentions, although such intentions are important. Discipline and consistent practice of the new skills are required. We adults find that deeply rooted habit patterns are hard to shake, and most of us resist repetitious practice. We often assume that, as adults, we are beyond the need to practice tedious skills (unless they are related to sports, the arts, or hobbies.) Yet sustained change comes only when new habits begin to replace old habits. If our barnyard eagle had chosen to soar through the skies, his first attempts would likely leave something to be desired. With practice, however, he could release the innate capacity stored deep within. It's the same for us. To experience this life-giving process more fully, we must begin with the small steps that validate and dignify our innate worth.

Six key skills foster creative interchange and transform life and work:

1. **Advocating with integrity from your original self.**

2. **Inquiring with humility into the originality of others.**

3. **Finding the positive values and drawbacks in any idea, belief, or perspective.**

4. **Seeking the "yes/and" for integrating diverse perspectives.**

5. **Acting on the best you've learned.**

6. **Committing to creative transformation.**

We Have A Choice

Freeing oneself from the vicious circle and practicing creative interchange skills are ultimately one and the same process. Creative interchange is incompatible with the vicious circle. Just as the vicious circle obstructs creative interchange, creative interchange releases us from the vicious circle. The more often we intentionally and consistently engage in creative interchange, the fewer times we will relapse into the vicious circle. The more I interact authentically with the intent to appreciatively understand my boss, spouse, child, or friend, the more I can creatively integrate and continue improving my personal, interpersonal, team, organizational, and community relationships.

Certainly, the ideal world is one in which everyone engages in this process consistently. If that were reality, the sharing, understanding, appreciating, and building on one another's best would be reciprocal. Unfortunately, our world is not ideal. As human beings, we all have moments when we fall back into the vicious circle. We have yet to find anyone who has permanently escaped the crippling dynamics of the vicious circle in his or her life. And, for whatever reason, some people are more vulnerable to this destructive spiral than others.

That doesn't matter. As Gandhi so wisely observed, the process begins with each of us. We always have a choice: we can live like a caged animal according to our constructed self, working endlessly to meet demands and expectations without being satisfied; or we can risk sharing our creative self openly with others. The worst that can happen is that someone will reject us. When this occurs, we must remember that the rejection is a message about that person's unfulfilled demands, rather than a truth about us. The process is simple, the outcome profound.

16

Released for Flight

*"One can never consent to creep
when one feels an impulse to soar."*

— Helen Keller

The next from the Flock came Kirk Maynard Gull, wobbling across the sand, dragging his left wing, to collapse at Jonathan's feet. "Help me," he said very quietly, speaking in the way that the dying speak. "I want to fly more than anything else in the world . . ."

"Come along then," said Jonathan. "Climb with me away from the ground, and we'll begin."

"You don't understand. My wing. I can't move my wing."

"Maynard Gull, you have the freedom to be yourself, your true self, here and now, and nothing can stand in your way. It is the Law of the Great Gull, the Law that Is."

"Are you saying I can fly?"

"I say you are free."

As simply and as quickly as that, Kirk Maynard Gull spread his wings, effortlessly, and lifted into the dark night air. The Flock was roused from sleep by his cry, as loud as he could scream it, from five hundred feet up: "I can fly! Listen! I CAN FLY!"

— *Richard Bach*, Jonathan Livingston Seagull

Released for Flight

We began this book with a story about an eagle who believed he was a chicken. Though he admired the majestic eagle he observed in flight, the illusion he had grown up with doomed him to live out his days clucking and scratching for feed. He never knew that he, too, could spread his wings and soar through the sky.

Now we read from *Jonathan Livingston Seagull* a similar story. Accepting yourself and believing you have the "freedom to be yourself, your true self" is the first requirement. This alone could have saved the eagle. Acceptance of your own inborn, unearned worth will also free you.

Let's take our bird metaphor one step further, with a last excerpt from Henry Nelson Wieman:

> Man is made for creative transformation as a bird is made for flight. To be sure he is in a cage much of the time. The bars of the cage are the resistances to creative transformation which are present in himself and in the world round about. Also, like most birds when long confined, he settles down in time and loses . . . the desire . . . to undergo creative transformation.
>
> — *Man's Ultimate Commitment*

The underlying cause of our confinement is the illusion of our lack of worth, a learned inability to accept our inborn capacity to participate in transforming creativity. Worth is given, not performance-based as we have grown to believe. We had worth at birth, when our performance track record was nonexistent. Now we are ready to rediscover what we've never lost. We are ready to stop searching for our worth outside ourselves, for it simply isn't there and never was there. No one else can give you worth. You were born with the capacity for creative transformation. No one can give you what you already have, and no one can ever take it away.

Acceptance of worth is the key to unlocking the cage and learning that you can, with practice, do far more than fly a few feet off the ground, cluck, and scratch in the barnyard for worms. While this is simple advice, it is extremely hard to realize. Our creative selves are buried under years of habit developed in the construction of the false self. You know the saying, "Old habits die hard." People find it difficult to put forth the effort to rediscover their capacity for creative transformation while they are yet laboring under the illusion that they lack the worth to pursue such a discovery. And the most subtle and ironic aspect of the journey is that many of us who begin the effort to claim our worth make that worth conditional on our success. The grip of the vicious circle is strong — as strong as death — for it leads to spiritual, physical, and emotional death unless we succeed in flying free.

The good news is, creative interchange is even stronger. Engaging in creative interchange opens the cage door to free the eagle within. The power of this process to liberate human beings is immense. As we travel in our work as consultants, helping people to understand the vicious circle and learn to engage more intentionally and consistently in creative interchange, we see powerful transformations take place. We know it is possible. There's a world of evidence to support the reality.

Although we will not escape the vicious circle indefinitely, occasional feelings of inadequacy and sorrow can serve as a wake-up call to remind us of the untapped, transforming power within. Rather than focusing on our ailments, grievances, and complaints that life has not given us the happiness we believe we deserve, we can view life, with George Bernard Shaw, as "a splendid torch" that we can "burn as brightly as possible before handing it on to future generations" *(Man and Superman)*.

By knowing what imprisons us, we can begin to unlock our cages and become uniquely and most fully who we are. Consider this your invitation to begin.

> *"Come to the edge," he said.*
> *They said, "We are afraid."*
> *"Come to the edge," he said.*
> *They came.*
> *He pushed them*
> *And they flew.*
>
> — Guillaume Apollinaire

To Find Out More

SynerChange

SynerChange is a consulting firm based in Atlanta, Georgia, and serving leaders and organizations throughout the world. The company's sole purpose is facilitation of the conscious and consistent practice of Creative InterChange™. Creative InterChange™ is the unique process at the foundation of meaningful and constructive human inter-action — whether that be consulting, leading, teaming, coaching, managing, or problem solving. "SynerChange" means "together change." The SynerChange family of companies includes offices in Chicago, Antwerp, and Helsinki.

SynerChange offers speaking engagements, seminars, management consultation, and mentoring for senior management. SynerChange interventions address leadership development, strategic thinking, optimizing team performance, innovative problem solving, diversity, corporate ethics, and organizational change. SynerChange works with a wide range of businesses and institutions, including the church, government, families, and education. Stacie and Charlie are available for speaking engagements on *The Chicken Conspiracy* and Creative InterChange™.

If you'd like to learn more or simply want to share your reflections on this book, please contact Stacie and Charlie at:

SynerChange
P.O. Box 942231
Atlanta, GA 31141
Phone: 404-297-9388

Or contact us through our web site at:
www.synerchange.com

About The Authors

Stacie S. Hagan

Stacie Hagan, Co-founder/President/CEO of SynerChange, is an international consultant to senior executives and top management. Through her entrepreneurial spirit and vision, affiliate offices of SynerChange have been established in Chicago, Antwerp, and Helsinki. Stacie speaks and conducts seminars regularly with client groups from the Americas, Europe, Australia, and Asia. She is a graduate of Yale University.

One of the world's leading authorities on the process of Creative InterChange™, Stacie founded the Center for Creative InterChange to help six major institutions — government, business and industry, education, family, healthcare, and the church — rediscover and claim the power of the Creative InterChange™ process. Those who know her describe Stacie as the "embodiment" of Creative InterChange™, someone who listens to you "as if you're the only person in the world."

Whether you find Stacie in executive meetings with clients, delivering speeches and workshops, working with her husband in the yard, or driving carpool with the children, her commitment to a life of balance is apparent. Stacie lives in Atlanta, Georgia, with her husband, Jim, two children, and their Golden Retriever.

About The Authors

Charlie Palmgren, Ph.D.

Charlie Palmgren, Co-founder/ Senior Partner of SynerChange, is an international consultant to corporate leaders and business consultants in a wide range of industries. Throughout a 35-year practice, Charlie's research and experience have focused on the conditions for Creative InterChange™. It isn't uncommon for Charlie to answer the phone and hear the voice of a client or colleague from 20–30 years ago. "The successes are revealed," Charlie states, "when people call decades later to say, 'You changed my life.'"

In the course of his career, Charlie has written and co-written articles, contributed to a book on Creative InterChange™, and acted as a consultant to the White House. His experience also includes such roles as personal and family counselor, drug prevention program director, medical school professor, and leader of public education reform.

On most evenings, Charlie can be found climbing Stone Mountain near his home in Georgia where he lives with his wife of 41 years, Marian, and their two cats. Charlie has four married children and ten grandchildren.

About The Illustrator

Sarah Minor

Sarah Minor, professional illustrator and graphic designer, is founder of Minor Details, a Columbia, Missouri–based design firm specializing in the "minor details that make a major difference." Sarah works in various media to help organizations, authors, and advertisers communicate their message in creative and original ways. Her many accomplishments include children's book illustrations, award-winning watercolor paintings, and business logos for companies in the United States and Europe. Sarah lives in Columbia, Missouri, with her husband, two daughters, and her cat.

Recovery Communications, Inc.

BOOK PUBLISHING & AUTHOR PROMOTIONS
Post Office Box 19910 • Baltimore, Maryland 21211, USA

Now available through your local bookstore!

Jennifer J. Richardson, M.S.W. *Diary of Abuse/Diary of Healing.* A young girl's secret journal recording two decades of abuse, with detailed healing therapy sessions. A very raw and extraordinary book. **Contact the author at: (404) 373-1837.**

Toby Rice Drews. *Getting Them Sober, Volume One — You Can Help!* Hundreds of ideas for sobriety and recovery. The million-seller endorsed by Melody Beattie, Dr. Norman Vincent Peale, and "Dear Abby." **Contact the author at: (410) 243-8352.**

Toby Rice Drews. *Getting Them Sober, Volume Four — Separation Decisions.* All about detachment and separation issues for families of alcoholics. Endorsed by Max Weisman, M.D., past president of the American Society of Addiction Medicine. **Contact the author at: (410) 243-8352.**

Betsy Tice White. *Turning Your Teen Around — How A Couple Helped Their Troubled Son While Keeping Their Marriage Alive and Well.* A doctor family's successful personal battle against teen-age drug use, with dozens of powerfully helpful tips for parents in pain. Endorsed by John Palmer, NBC News. **Contact the author at: (770) 590-7311.**

Betsy Tice White. *Mountain Folk, Mountain Food — Down-Home Wisdom, Plain Tales, and Recipe Secrets from Appalachia.* The joy of living as expressed in charming vignettes and mouth-watering regional foods! Endorsed by the host of the TV series "Great Country Inns" and by *Blue Ridge Country Magazine.* **Contact the author at: (770) 590-7311.**

Linda Meyer, Ph.D. *I See Myself Changing — Weekly Meditations and Recovery Journaling for Young Adults.* A life-affirming book for adolescents and young adults, endorsed by Robert Bulkeley, The Gilman School. **Contact the author at: (217) 367-8821.**

Joseph L. Buccilli, Ph.D. *Wise Stuff About Relationships.* A gem of a book for anyone in recovery; "an empowering spiritual workout." Endorsed by the vice president of the *Philadelphia Inquirer.* **Contact the author at: (609) 629-4441.**

John Pearson. *Eastern Shore Beckonings.* Marvelous trek back in time through charming villages and encounters with solid Chesapeake Bay folk. "Aches with affection" — the *Village Voice's* Washington correspondent. **Contact the author at: (410) 315-7940.**

Jerry Zeller. *The Shaman and Other Almost-Tall Tales.* Enchanting storytelling and grace-filled character sketches from an Episcopal archdeacon and former Emory University dean. **Contact the author at: (706) 692-5842.**

AND COMING SOON . . . .

Mattie Carroll Mullins. *Judy — The Murder of My Daughter, The Healing of My Family.* A Christian mother's inspiring story of how her family moved from unimaginable tragedy to forgiveness.

David E. Bergesen. *Murder Crosses the Equator — A Father Jack Carthier Mystery.* Volcanic tale of suspense in a Latin-American setting, starring a clever missionary-priest detective.